McGRAW-HILL
SCIENCE

Macmillan/McGraw-Hill Edition

Richard Moyer ● **Lucy Daniel** ● **Jay Hackett**

H. Prentice Baptiste ● **Pamela Stryker** ● **JoAnne Vasquez**

NATIONAL
GEOGRAPHIC
SOCIETY

On the Cover:
This black bear cub, native to North America, was born
in January or February and weighed less than a pound. An
adult male usually weighs between 90 and 135 kilograms
(200 and 300 pounds). But one weighed in at 236 kilograms
(520 pounds). Black bears fatten up on fruit and then
often sleep through the winter's coldest weather.

Mc Graw Hill **Macmillan McGraw-Hill**

New York   **Farmington**

Program Authors

Dr. Lucy H. Daniel
Teacher, Consultant
Rutherford County Schools, North Carolina

Dr. Jay Hackett
Professor Emeritus of Earth Sciences
University of Northern Colorado

Dr. Richard H. Moyer
Professor of Science Education
University of Michigan-Dearborn

Dr. H. Prentice Baptiste
Professor of Science and Multicultural Education
New Mexico State University
Las Cruces, New Mexico

Pamela Stryker, M.Ed.
Elementary Educator and Science Consultant
Eanes Independent School District
Austin, Texas

Dr. JoAnne Vasquez
Elementary Science Education Consultant
Mesa Public Schools, Arizona
NSTA Past President

NATIONAL
GEOGRAPHIC
SOCIETY
Washington, D.C.

The features in this textbook entitled "Who's a Scientist?" "Amazing Stories," and "People in Science," as well as the unit openers, were developed in collaboration with the National Geographic Society's School Publishing Division.

Copyright © 2002 National Geographic Society. All rights reserved.

The name "National Geographic" and the Yellow Border are registered trademarks of the National Geographic Society.

Macmillan/McGraw-Hill

A Division of The McGraw·Hill Companies

Macmillan/McGraw-Hill
Two Penn Plaza
New York, New York 10121-2298

Printed in the United States of America

ISBN 0-02-280034-4 / 1

1 2 3 4 5 6 7 8 9 107 07 06 05 04 03 02 01

Teacher Reviewers

Peoria, IL
Rolling Acres Middle School
Gail Truho

Rockford, IL
Rockford Public Schools
Dr. Sharon Wynstra
Science Coordinator

Newark, NJ
Alexander Street School
Cheryl Simeonidis

Albuquerque, NM
Jackie Costales
Science Coordinator, Montgomery Complex

Poughkeepsie, NY
St. Peter's School
Monica Crolius

Columbus, OH
St. Mary's School
Linda Cotter
Joby Easley

Keizer, OR
Cummings Elementary
Deanna Havel

McMinnville, OR
McMinnville School District
Kristin Ward

Salem, OR
Fruitland Elementary
   Mike Knudson

Four Corners Elementary
   Bethany Ayers
   Sivhong Hanson
   Cheryl Kirkelie
   Julie Wells

Salem-Keizer Public Schools
   Rachael Harms
   Sue Smith,
   Science Specialist

Yoshikai Elementary
   Joyce Davenport

Norristown, PA
St. Teresa of Avila
Fran Fiordimondo

Pittsburgh, PA
Chartiers Valley Intermediate School
Rosemary Hutter

Memphis, TN
Memphis City Schools
Quincy Hathorn
District Science Facilitator

Consultants

Dr. Carol Baskin
University of Kentucky
Lexington, KY

Dr. Joe W. Crim
University of Georgia
Athens, GA

Dr. Marie DiBerardino
Allegheny University of
Health Sciences
Philadelphia, PA

Dr. R. E. Duhrkopf
Baylor University
Waco, TX

Dr. Dennis L. Nelson
Montana State University
Bozeman, MT

Dr. Fred Sack
Ohio State University
Columbus, OH

Dr. Martin VanDyke
Denver, CO

Dr. E. Peter Volpe
Mercer University
Macon, GA

Consultants

Dr. Clarke Alexander
Skidaway Institute of
Oceanography
Savannah, GA

Dr. Suellen Cabe
Pembroke State University
Pembroke, NC

Dr. Thomas A. Davies
Texas A & M University
College Station, TX

Dr. Ed Geary
Geological Society of America
Boulder, CO

Dr. David C. Kopaska-Merkel
Geological Survey of Alabama
Tuscaloosa, AL

Consultants

Dr. Bonnie Buratti
Jet Propulsion Lab
Pasadena, CA

Dr. Shawn Carlson
Society of Amateur Scientists
San Diego, CA

Dr. Karen Kwitter
Williams College
Williamstown, MA

Dr. Steven Souza
Williamstown, MA

Dr. Joseph P. Straley
University of Kentucky
Lexington, KY

Dr. Thomas Troland
University of Kentucky
Lexington, KY

Dr. Josephine Davis Wallace
University of North Carolina
Charlotte, NC

Consultant for Primary Grades

Donna Harrell Lubcker
East Texas Baptist University
Marshall, TX

Teacher Panelists

Newark, NJ
First Avenue School
Jorge Alameda
Concetta Cioci
Neva Galasso
Bernadette Kazanjian-reviewer
Toby Marks
Janet Mayer-reviewer
Maria Tutela

Brooklyn, NY
P.S. 31
  Janet Mantel
  Paige McGlone
  Madeline Pappas
  Maria Puma-reviewer
P.S. 217
  Rosemary Ahern
  Charles Brown
  Claudia Deeb-reviewer
  Wendy Lerner
P.S. 225
  Christine Calafiore
  Annette Fisher-reviewer

P.S. 250
  Melissa Kane
P.S. 277
  Erica Cohen
  Helena Conti
  Anne Marie Corrado
  Deborah Scott-DiClemente
  Jeanne Fish
  Diane Fromhartz
  Tricia Hinz
  Lisa Iside
  Susan Malament
  Joyce Menkes-reviewer
  Elaine Noto
  Jean Pennacchio
Jeffrey Hampton
Mwaka Yavana

Elmont, NY
Covert Avenue School
Arlene Connelly

Mt. Vernon, NY
Holmes School
Jennifer Cavallaro
Lou Ciofi
George DiFiore
Brenda Durante
Jennifer Hawkins-reviewer
Michelle Mazzotta
Catherine Moringiello
Mary Jane Oria-reviewer
Lucille Pierotti
Pia Vicario-reviewer

Ozone Park, NY
St. Elizabeth School
Joanne Cocchiola-reviewer
Helen DiPietra-reviewer
Barbara Kingston
Madeline Visco

St. Albans, NY
Orvia Williams

UNIT A

Life Science

Plants Are Living Things PAGE A1

Who's a Scientist? PAGE S1

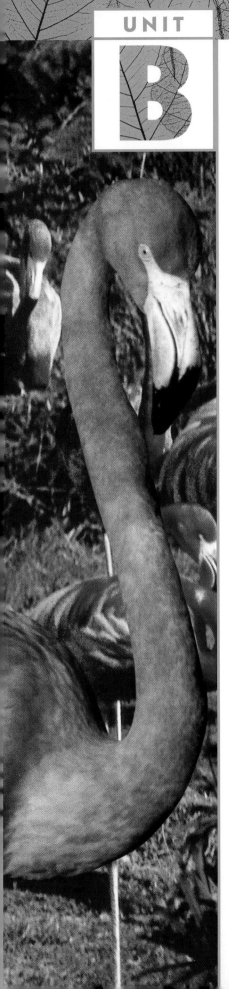

Life Science

UNIT B

Animals Are Living Things PAGE B1

v

UNIT C

Earth Science

The Sky and Weather PAGE C1

Caring for Earth PAGE D1

Matter, Matter Everywhere **PAGE E1**

Physical Science

On the Move PAGE F1

Read these pages. They will help you understand this book.

This is the name of the lesson.

Get Ready asks a question to get you started. You can answer the question from the picture.

This Science Skill is used in the Explore Activity.

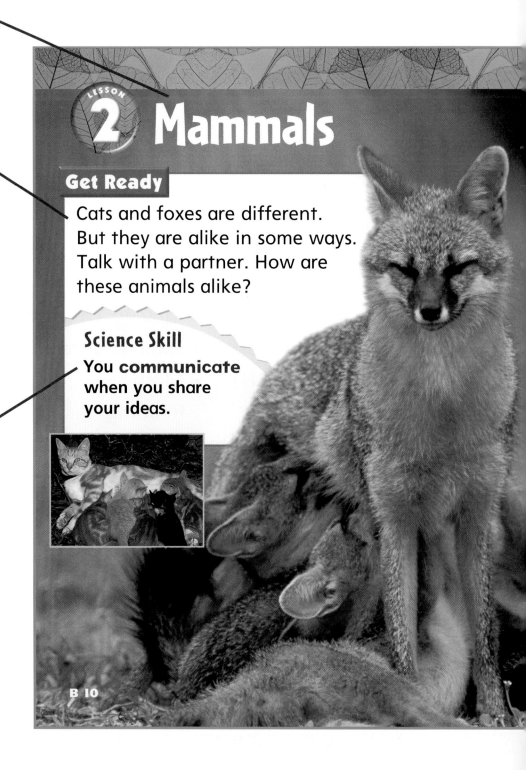

LESSON
2 Mammals

Get Ready

Cats and foxes are different. But they are alike in some ways. Talk with a partner. How are these animals alike?

Science Skill

You **communicate** when you share your ideas.

B 10

You can try the **Explore Activity** before you read the lesson.

The **Explore Activity** helps you answer a question.

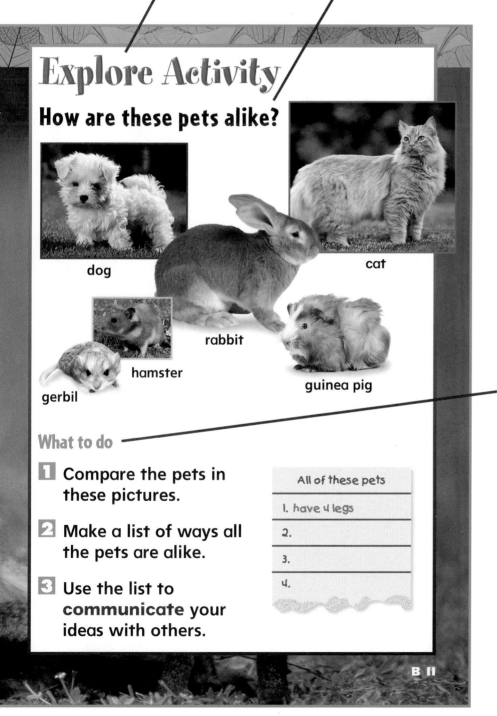

Explore Activity

How are these pets alike?

dog

cat

rabbit

hamster

gerbil

guinea pig

What to do are the steps you follow.

What to do

1. Compare the pets in these pictures.

2. Make a list of ways all the pets are alike.

3. Use the list to **communicate** your ideas with others.

All of these pets
1. have 4 legs
2.
3.
4.

B 11

Now you are ready to read

Before You Read
Read the red question at the top of the page. It will help you find the main idea.

Dark words with yellow around them are new words to learn.

Read
As you read, look for the answer.

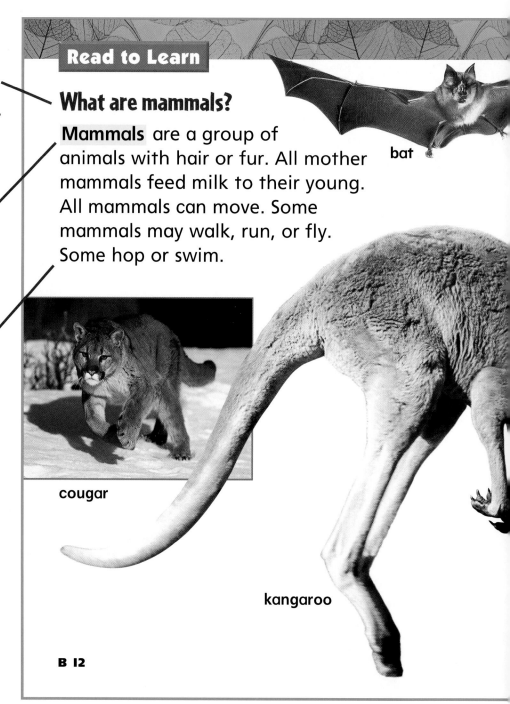

Read to Learn

What are mammals?

Mammals are a group of animals with hair or fur. All mother mammals feed milk to their young. All mammals can move. Some mammals may walk, run, or fly. Some hop or swim.

bat

cougar

kangaroo

B 12

This label tells you what the picture is. Pictures and words work together.

seal

Bats, cats, and seals are mammals. You know another mammal—you! That's right, people are mammals, too.

▷ **How are mammals alike?**

human

After You Read
This question helps you check what you just read.

These questions check what you learned in the lesson.

Stop and Think

1. What do mammals feed their young?
2. What makes people mammals?

MORE TO READ Read **Baby Whales Drink Milk** by Barbara Juster Esbensen.

Fun activities help you learn more.

B 13

Wash your hands after each activity.

Read all steps a few times before you start.

When you see this:

BE CAREFUL!

you should be careful.

Be careful with glass and sharp objects.

Cover your clothes or wear old ones.

Listen to the teacher.

Never taste or smell anything unless your teacher tells you to.

Keep your workplace neat. Clean up after you are done.

Tell the teacher about accidents and spills right away.

Wear goggles when you are told to.

SCIENCE Safety OUTDOORS

Don't touch plants or animals unless your teacher tells you to.

Tell the teacher about accidents right away.

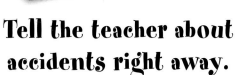

Listen to the teacher.

Never taste or smell anything unless your teacher tells you to.

Stay with your group.

Never throw your trash on the ground.

Put living things back where you found them.

Who's a Scientist?

NATIONAL GEOGRAPHIC

Look and see.

Who's a Scientist?

There are many kinds of scientists.
You can be one, too.

A Scientist:

- observes
- compares
- measures
- classifies things
- makes a model
- communicates
- infers
- puts things in order
- predicts
- investigates
- draws a conclusion

Scientists observe.

Look for a red rock.
Tell what you might
hear at this pond.

Scientists compare and measure.

Compare these lines.
Measure them.
Which one is longest?

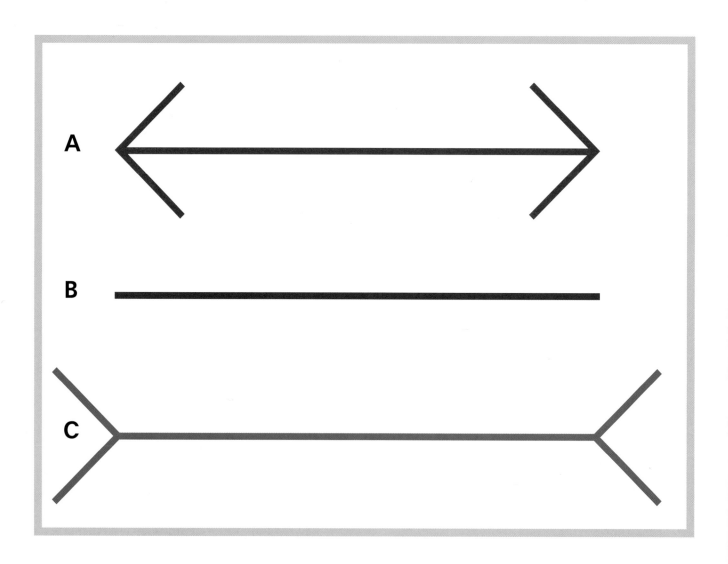

Scientists classify things.

In which group does this belong?
How do you know?
See! You are a scientist, too!

Scientists make models.

Make a model airplane.
How well did it fly?

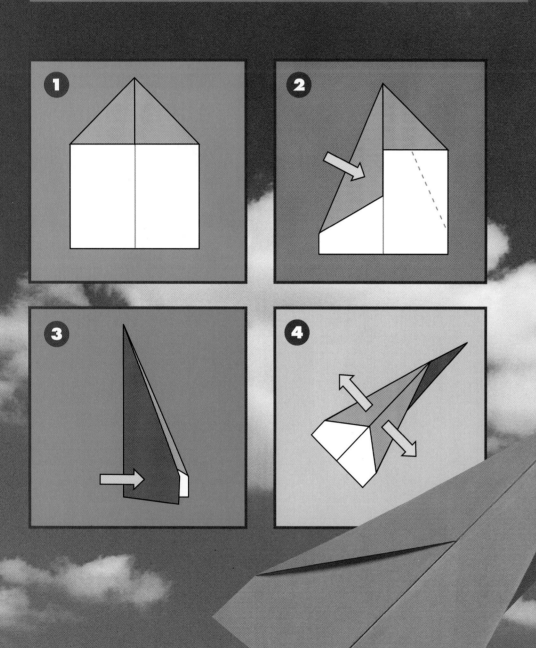

Scientists communicate.

What is missing from this picture?
Tell others your answer.

Scientists infer.

Where have these children been?
What clues help you know?

Scientists put things in order.

Put these pictures in order.

Scientists predict.

Predict what will happen next.
You are a scientist, too.

Scientists investigate and draw conclusions.

Investigate these tracks.
Which animal made them?

UNIT A
Plants Are Living Things

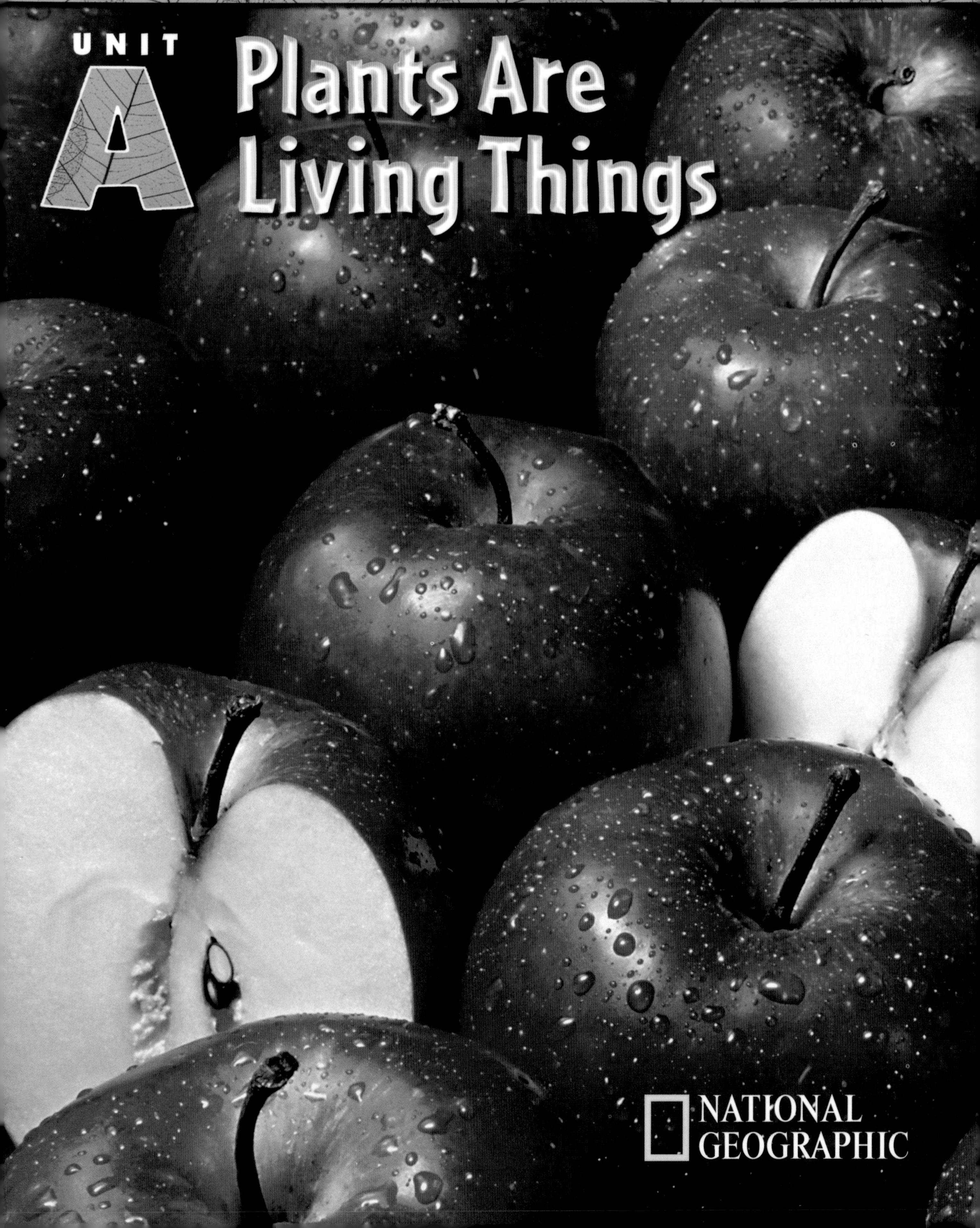

Plants Are Living Things

LOOK!

Tell about this fruit.
What color is it?
Where did it come from?
Take a good look!

CHAPTER 1

All About Living Things

Did You Ever Wonder?

What is alive? The child is alive. Her hat is not. The flowers are alive. The dirt below is not. What else is alive?

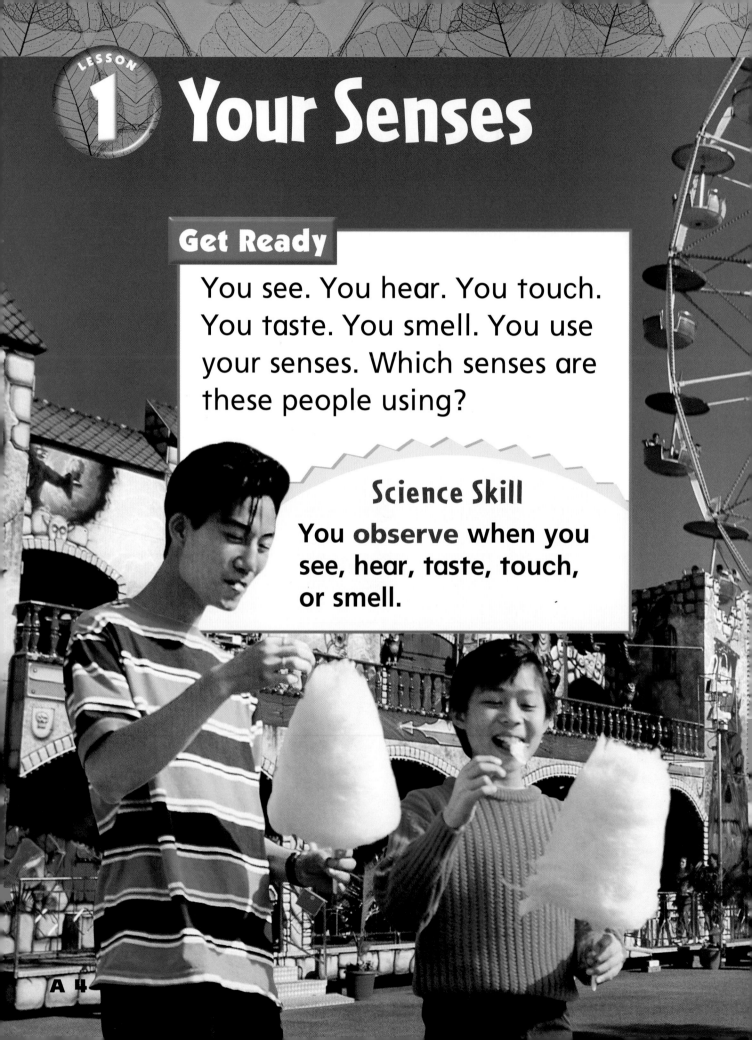

Your Senses

Get Ready

You see. You hear. You touch. You taste. You smell. You use your senses. Which senses are these people using?

Science Skill

You **observe** when you see, hear, taste, touch, or smell.

Explore Activity

What do you observe?

What to do

ball

sponge

1 Look at each thing. What do you see?

2 Touch each thing. How does it feel?

3 What do you **observe** about the ball and the sponge? Tell about each one.

How do you see and hear?

You have five **senses**. Your senses help you find out about the world around you.

You see with your eyes. When you see, you find out how things look.

▷ **What does the child see?**

You use your ears to hear.
When you hear, you find
out how things sound.

**?▷ What makes a
softer sound?**

How do you taste, touch, and smell?

When you taste, you find out about the foods you eat.

You use your nose to smell.

▷ **How does the flower smell?**

▷ **How does the fruit taste?**

A 8

When you touch things, you find out how they feel.

▶ **How does the paint feel?**

Stop and Think

1. What are your five senses?
2. Which senses do you use when you eat?

MORE TO READ Read **My Five Senses** by Margaret Miller.

Living and Nonliving Things

Get Ready

Which dog is living?
Which one is not living?
How do you know?

Science Skill

You **compare** when you observe how things are alike and how they are different.

Explore Activity

How do a rock and a caterpillar compare?

What to do

1 Observe the rock and the caterpillar. Use the hand lens. **Compare** what they do.

2 Put the rock, the food, and the caterpillar into the box. Wash your hands.

3 Compare the rock and the caterpillar in a few days. What do you observe?

What are living things?

Living things grow and change. They need air, food, and water to grow and change. All living things make other living things like themselves. Animals, plants, and people are living things.

water

air

food

▷ **What things here are living? Tell how you know.**

What are nonliving things?

Nonliving things do not grow. They do not need air, food, or water. They do not make other things like themselves. Cars and rocks are nonliving things.

> **How do you know these things are nonliving?**

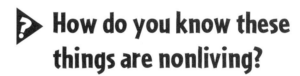

Stop and Think

1. What are some living things?

2. How can you tell if something is nonliving?

 **HOME ACTIVITY** Go on a scavenger hunt with an adult. Find three living things. Find three nonliving things.

A 13

Make a Touch Picture

We use the sense of touch to learn about things.

Try This!

Make a touch picture. Find things that feel different. Glue them onto paper. Have others close their eyes. Let them touch your picture. Can they tell what each thing is?

Science Newsroom CD-ROM
Choose **Skeleton Key** to learn more about living things.

A Japanese Garden

Some gardens in Japan look like this one. It has living and nonliving things in it. This garden is a quiet place.

Try This!

Draw a garden like the one above. Show living and nonliving things in it. Show your drawing to others.

Vocabulary

living thing

nonliving thing

Use the words from the box to tell about items 1–4.

1

2

3

4

Science Ideas

Which senses do the children use here?

5

6

7

8 Tell which body parts you use when you see, hear, touch, taste, and smell.

Science Skill: Observe

What can you observe about each thing?

9

10

11

12

2 A Look at Plants

Vocabulary

roots

stem

trunk

leaves

seed

seedling

flowers

fruit

Did You Ever Wonder?

How big do some plants get? A pumpkin can get very big. It can be as heavy as a horse! These people made boats from pumpkins. How else do people use plants?

A 19

Plants Are Living Things

Get Ready

Look at this plant. It is getting something it needs. What is it?

Science Skill

You **observe** when you look, see, hear, touch, taste, or smell something.

Explore Activity

What happens to a plant that does not get water?

What to do

1. Place both plants in a sunny place.

2. Water one plant. Do not water the other one.

3. **Observe** the plants for a week. What happens to each plant? Draw any changes you see.

What do plants need to live?

Plants are living things. Plants need water and air. If they do not get these things, they can not live.

water

no water

Plants make their own food. They make food from water and air. Plants must have light to make food. They also need what is in soil to grow.

▶ **What will happen to a plant that does not get what it needs?**

light

no light

Where can you find plants?

You can find plants almost everywhere. Plants grow where they get what they need to live.

dry, hot place

cold place

Some plants grow in cold places.
Some plants grow in hot places.
Some grow where it is wet.
And some grow where it is dry.

? **Where do these plants live?**

wet place

Stop and Think

1. What do plants need to live?
2. Why can plants grow in different kinds of places?

HOME ACTIVITY

Find plants where you live. Go with an adult. Talk about where plants grow.

Get Ready

Look closely. How are these plants alike? How are they different?

Science Skill

You **compare** when you observe how things are alike and different.

Explore Activity

How are plant parts alike and different?

What to do

1 Look at the plants. Use a hand lens. Draw a picture of each one. Wash your hands.

2 **Compare** your drawings. Do the plants have parts that are alike? Circle them. Talk about it.

3 How are the parts different? Talk about it.

unpotted radish plant

unpotted mum plant

crayons

drawing paper

hand lens

What parts do plants have?

Most plants have roots, stems, and leaves. Most roots grow under the soil. Stems and leaves grow above the soil.

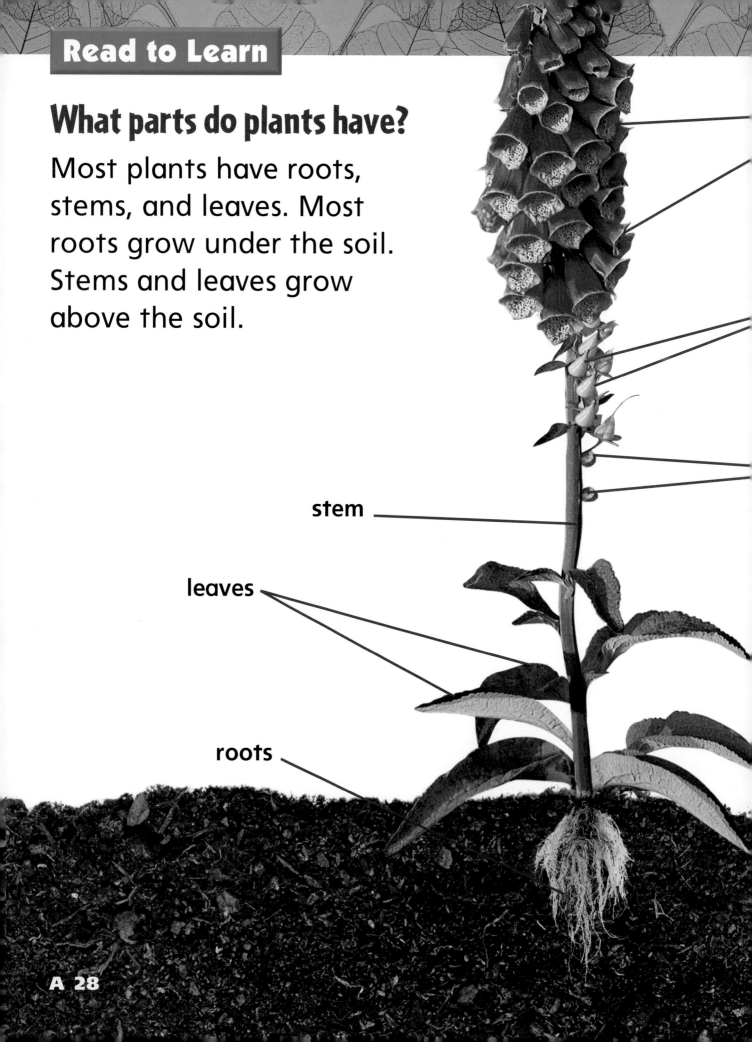

stem

leaves

roots

flowers

fruits

seeds

Most plants also have seeds. Most seeds come from flowers. Flowers grow into fruits. Fruits have seeds inside.

▷ **What plant parts of the daisy do you see?**

daisy

Stop and Think

1. What parts do most plants have?

2. Where do most seeds come from?

AT THE COMPUTER

Visit **www.mhscience02.com** to learn more about plants.

Get Ready

The wind blows hard. But the tree does not blow away. What keeps it in place? Tell how you know.

Science Skill

You **communicate** when you write, draw, or tell your ideas.

Explore Activity

What do you observe about roots?

plant

hand lens

newspaper

crayons

What to do

1. Gently pull the plant from the pot.

2. Look at the roots. Use the hand lens.

3. Draw a picture of the roots. **Communicate** what you observe about the roots. Wash your hands.

What do roots do?

Roots take in water for a plant.
They grow down into the soil.
They hold the plant in place.

dandelion with roots

Some roots grow deep into the soil.
Other roots do not grow deep.

▷ **Why are roots important?**

Stop and Think

1. What do roots do?
2. Do all roots look the same? Talk about it.

grass with roots

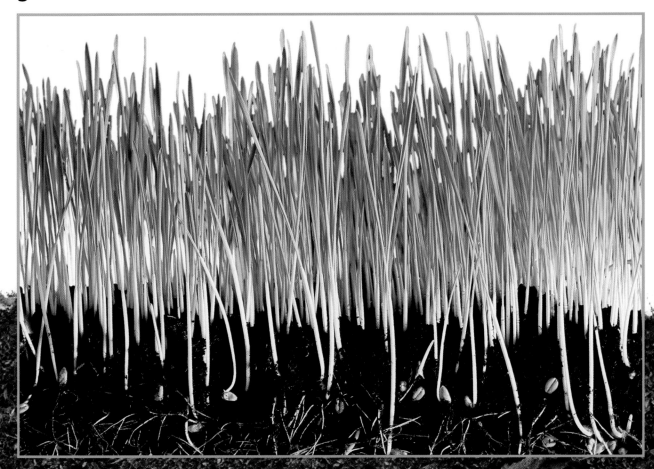

AT THE COMPUTER

Visit **www.mhscience02.com** to learn more about roots.

Stems and Leaves

Get Ready

These plants take in water. The water goes from the roots to all the plant's parts. How does it get there?

Science Skill

You **infer** when you use what you know to figure something out.

Explore Activity

How does water travel through a plant?

2 white flowers

jar of colored water

What to do

1 Put one flower in the jar of water.

2 Carefully bend the stem of the other flower. Put it in the jar. Wash your hands.

3 The next day, observe the flowers. **Infer** why this happens to each flower.

What do stems do?

Water and food move in a **stem** to other plant parts.

Water moves from the roots to the leaves. Food moves from the leaves to the roots and other parts.

daffodil

oak tree

A stem holds up a plant.
Some stems are green and thin.
Green stems may bend easily.
Some stems are dark and thick.
They do not bend easily. The stem
of a tree is called a **trunk**.

▷ **How are these stems alike?**
How are they different?

rose

vine

What do leaves do?

Leaves make food for a plant. Leaves take in air and use light to make food. They also use water from the soil.

maple
leaf

swiss cheese
leaf

buckeye
leaf

maple tree

pine tree

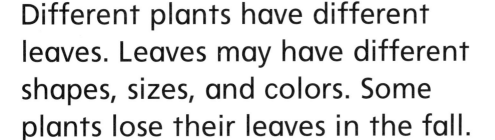
pine leaf

Different plants have different leaves. Leaves may have different shapes, sizes, and colors. Some plants lose their leaves in the fall.

How are these leaves alike? How are they different?

Stop and Think

1. What do stems do?
2. What do leaves do?

honey suckle leaf

AT THE COMPUTER

Visit www.mhscience02.com to learn more about plants.

Seeds

Get Ready

Seeds do not all look the same. Tell how these seeds look different.

Science Skill

You **compare** when you observe how things are alike and different.

A 40

Explore Activity

How do seeds compare?

What you need

seeds

glue stick

hand lens

What to do

1. Observe the seeds. Use a hand lens.

2. **Compare** the seeds. Sort them into groups.

3. Glue each different kind of seed onto the chart. Fill in the chart. Wash your hands.

seed	color	shape	size	how it feels

seed

What is a seed?

A **seed** is the part of a plant that can grow into a new plant. Every seed has a tiny plant inside.

tiny plant

apples

A seed grows into the same kind of plant that it came from. An apple seed grows into an apple tree. A pumpkin seed grows into a pumpkin plant.

peas

pumpkins

▶ **What will grow from pea seeds?**

Stop and Think

1. What is inside a seed?

2. What will grow from a pine seed?

HOME ACTIVITY Make a fruit salad with an adult. What seeds can you see?

A 43

Plants Grow and Change

Get Ready

People plant seeds. They water them. What do you think will happen to the seeds?

Science Skill

You **predict** when you use what you know to tell what will happen.

Explore Activity

What do seeds need to grow?

What to do

seeds

1. Put one seed in a dry paper towel. Put the towel in a zipper bag.

paper towels

2. Put another seed in a wet paper towel. Put the towel in a zipper bag.

water

3. Place both bags in a warm place. **Predict** what will happen to each seed. Wash your hands.

hand lens

4. After a few days, observe both seeds. Use a hand lens. What do seeds need to grow?

plastic zipper bags

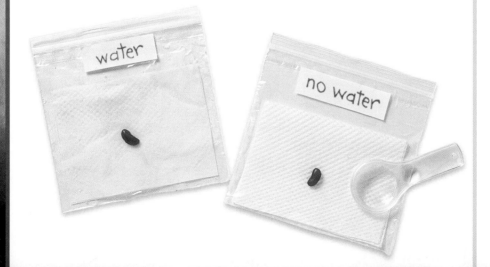

water

no water

How do seeds grow?

A seed grows when it gets water and warmth. First, it grows a tiny root. Next, it grows a stem and tiny leaves. The young plant is called a **seedling**.

The seed grows a root.

The seed grows more roots and sprouts a stem.

Leaves grow from the stem.

The seedling grows more roots and leaves. Its stem gets taller. Soon, it will be an adult plant. Then, the plant can make its own seeds.

Now the plant is a seedling.

> Tell how this seed grew.

How do plants make seeds?

Many plants grow **flowers**. The flowers make seeds. The **fruit** is the plant part that grows around the seeds. The fruit may fall to the ground. The seeds inside the fruit may grow into new plants.

The adult plant has flowers and fruits.

ponderosa pine cone

ponderosa pine tree

Not all plants grow flowers.
Pine trees grow pine cones.
Pine cones have seeds inside.

▷ **How is the pine tree different from the bean plant?**

Stop and Think

1. What does a seed need to grow?

2. What do flowers do?

MORE TO READ   Read **Garden** by Robert Maass.

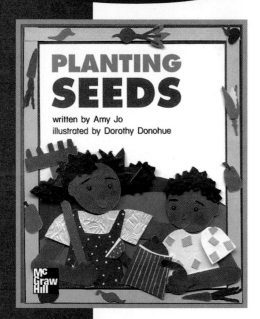

PLANTING
SEEDS

written by Amy Jo
illustrated by Dorothy Donohue

Plants We Eat

We eat some plants for food.
But we cannot eat all plants.
Find out about some seeds
people plant for food. Read
Planting Seeds by Amy Jo.

Try This!

Work with an adult.
Make a list of plants
we can eat. Make a
list of plants we can
not eat. Write or
draw the plants on
each list.

Watch It Grow!

As a bean seed grows, it changes. It gets taller. It grows more leaves.

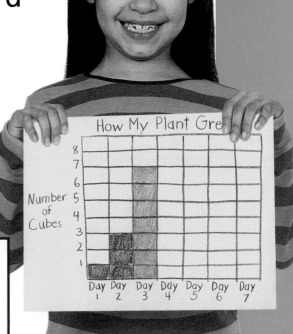

Try This!

Work with an adult. Plant a bean seed. Water it. Wait until it grows. Each day, measure how tall the plant is. Show how tall it gets in a graph.

 Science Newsroom CD-ROM Choose **Life of a Tree** to learn more about trees.

A 51

Vocabulary

fruit

stem

roots

seedling

seeds

flower

leaf

trunk

Use each word once for items 1–8. What does each picture show?

1

2

3

4

5

6

7

8

9 Tell what each part of this plant does.

10 Tell what happens in each picture.

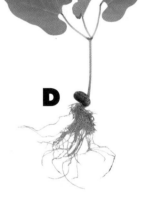

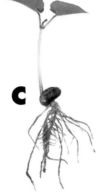

A **B** **C** **D**

11 Name two things plants need to live.

Science Skill: Compare

12 How are these leaves alike?

13 How are they different?

READ
Bit by Bit by Virginia Arnold

George Washington Carver

Plant Scientist

George Washington Carver was born a long time ago. He learned about plants as a child and in college. He became a plant scientist and a teacher.

George found many uses for peanuts. He used them to make shampoo and other things. Peanut plants help make the soil better. Better soil helps other plants grow well.

What did George Washington Carver find out?

George Washington Carver with students

SCIENCE
Workshop

1. Draw some pictures.
Be sure your pictures show:

- a nonliving thing you can see

- a nonliving thing you can hear

- a picture of yourself

Then write what you need to grow and change.

2. Draw a picture of an apple tree. Label the roots, stem, leaves, and fruit. Then write what is inside the fruit.

UNIT B
Animals Are Living Things

Animals Are Living Things

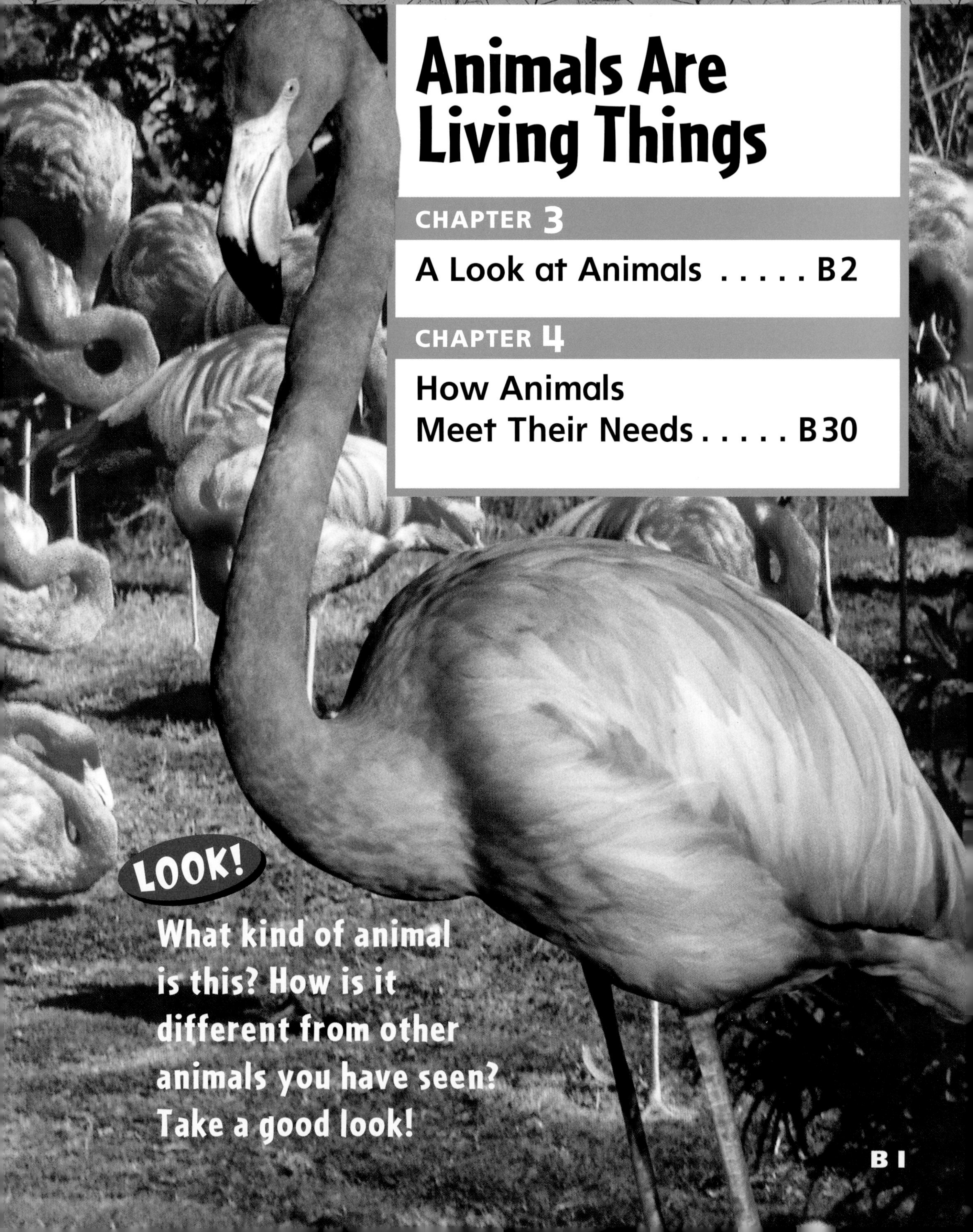

LOOK!

What kind of animal
is this? How is it
different from other
animals you have seen?
Take a good look!

3 A Look at Animals

Vocabulary

shelter
mammals
lungs
gills
amphibians
reptiles
insects
hatch
tadpoles

Did You Ever Wonder?

How do these cubs get what they need to grow? Their mother gives food to them. The cubs can not hunt until they are older. What else do the cubs need?

Animals Are Living Things

Get Ready

What is this parent bird doing? Are these birds living? How do you know?

Science Skill

You **infer** when you use what you know to figure something out.

Explore Activity

Are birds living things?

What to do

peanut
butter

1. Make a bird feeder with peanut butter and bird seed.

paper roll

2. Hang the bird feeder outside. Wash your hands.

bird seed

3. Observe the feeder each day. What do you see?

string

4. Can you **infer** that birds are living things? Talk about it.

craft stick

How are animals alike?

Animals are living things. They all need food, water, air, and a place to live. Animals come from other animals like themselves. They all grow and change.

parrots

water buffalo

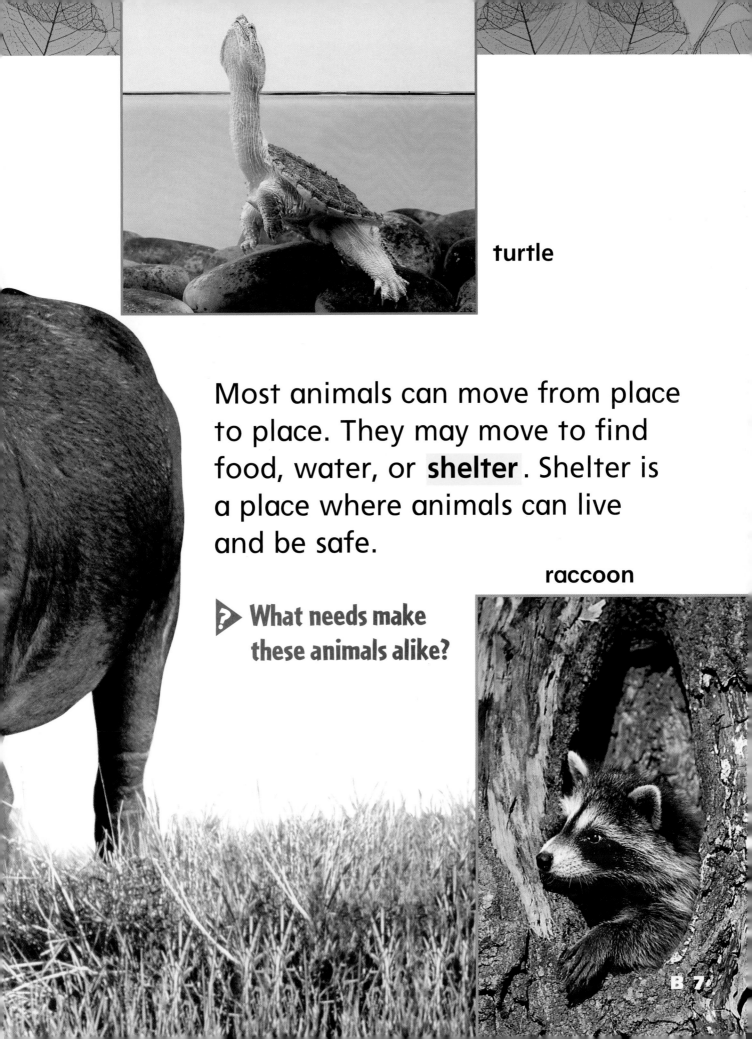

turtle

Most animals can move from place to place. They may move to find food, water, or **shelter**. Shelter is a place where animals can live and be safe.

raccoon

▶ **What needs make these animals alike?**

How are animals different?

Animals come in different
sizes. Some are big.
Some are small.

Animals have different
body coverings.
Some have fur.
Some have feathers.

bear

 moth

Animals have different numbers of legs. Some have six or more legs. Some have four legs. Some have two legs. And some have no legs at all.

▷ **How are these animals different?**

snake

goose

Stop and Think

1. In what ways are animals alike?

2. What are two ways that animals may be different?

HOME ACTIVITY Find pictures of animals. Tell how they are different.

Mammals

Get Ready

Cats and foxes are different.
But they are alike in some ways.
Talk with a partner. How are
these animals alike?

Science Skill

You **communicate**
when you share
your ideas.

Explore Activity

How are these pets alike?

dog

cat

rabbit

hamster

gerbil

guinea pig

What to do

1 Compare the pets in these pictures.

2 Make a list of ways all the pets are alike.

3 Use the list to **communicate** your ideas with others.

All of these pets
1. have 4 legs
2.
3.
4.

What are mammals?

Mammals are a group of animals with hair or fur. All mother mammals feed milk to their young. All mammals can move. Some mammals may walk, run, or fly. Some hop or swim.

bat

cougar

kangaroo

seal

Bats, cats, and seals are mammals. You know another mammal—you! That's right, people are mammals, too.

▶ **How are mammals alike?**

human

Stop and Think

1. What do mammals feed their young?

2. What makes people mammals?

MORE TO READ

Read **Baby Whales Drink Milk** by Barbara Juster Esbensen.

More Animal Groups

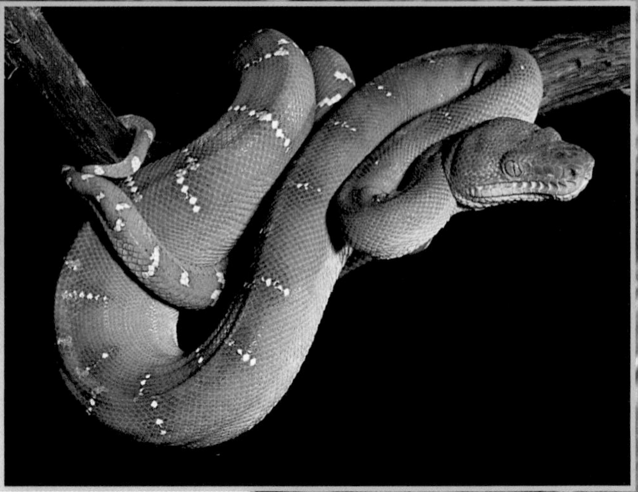

Get Ready

How are these animals alike? How can you group them?

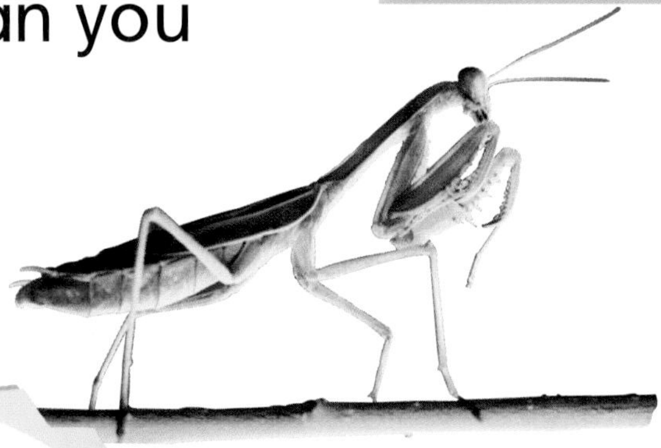

Science Skill

You **classify** when you group things by how they are alike.

Explore Activity

How can you classify animals?

toy animals

What to do

1 Look at the animals. Put them into groups. Draw sorting circles. Label each circle.

legs

no legs

2 Tell how all the animals in each group are alike.

3 Classify the animals in a different way. Make labels for your new groups.

What are birds?

Birds are animals with feathers. They have two legs and two wings. Most birds fly. They breathe with body parts called **lungs** .

eagle

bluebird

▷ **How are these birds different?**

duck

rhea

B 16

What are fish?

Fish live in water. They have fins that help them swim. Scales cover a fish's body. They breathe with body parts called **gills**.

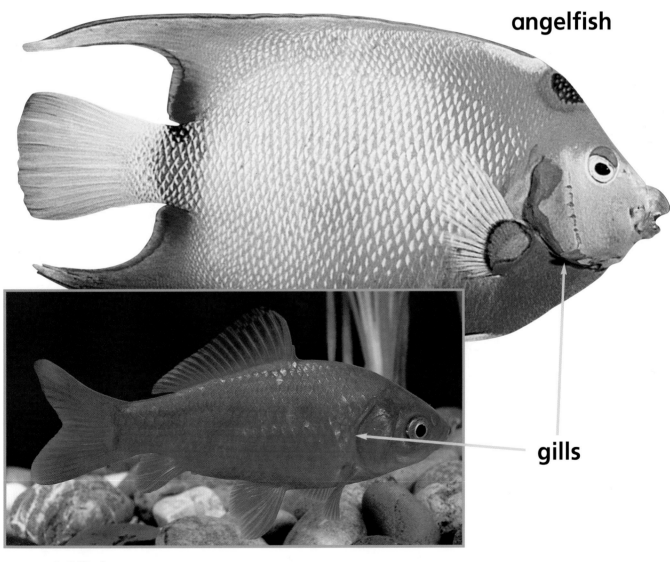

angelfish

gills

goldfish

▷ **How are these fish alike?**

What are amphibians?

Amphibians are animals that live in water and on land. Most have damp skin. A frog is an amphibian.

frog

What are reptiles?

Reptiles have dry skin that is covered with scales. Some reptiles also have shells. Turtles and snakes are reptiles.

turtle

▶ **What covers the frog, turtle, and snake?**

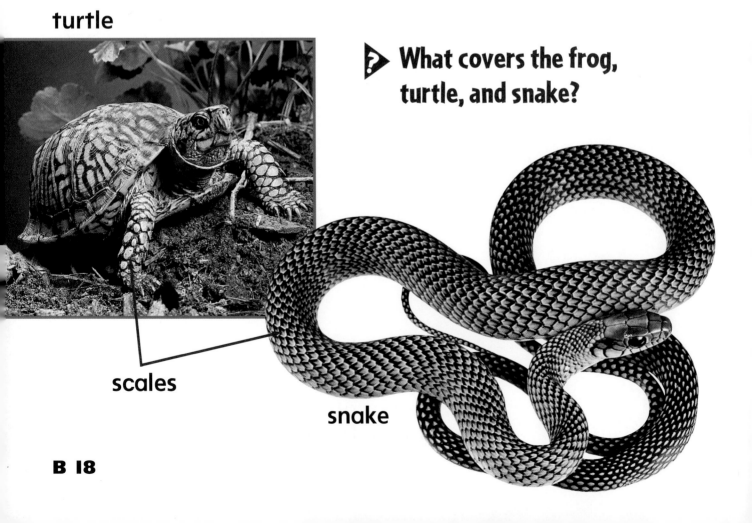

scales

snake

What are insects?

Insects are animals with three body parts and six legs. Most insects have hard body coverings. Most insects also have wings.

bee

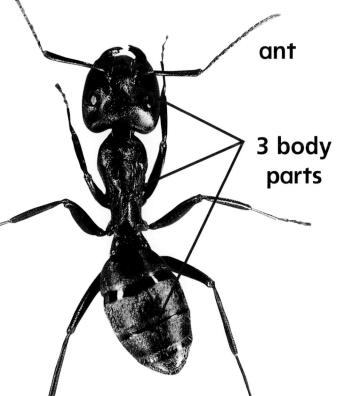

ant

3 body parts

▶ **Are these animals insects? Tell why.**

butterfly

Stop and Think

1. What are five animal groups?

2. What covers the bodies of the animals in each group?

Visit **www.mhscience02.com** to learn more about animals.

Grow and Change

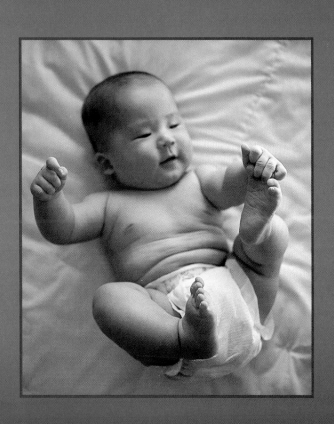

Get Ready

Look at these pictures.
How did this girl change?

Science Skill

You **compare** things when you tell how they are alike and different.

Explore Activity

How do animals change as they grow?

What to do

1 Pair each young animal with its parent.

2 **Compare** the animals in each pair. How did each animal change as it grew?

3 Which animal changed most?

How do some animals grow and change?

Young animals grow to look like their parents. When dogs are born, they can not see or walk. They drink their mother's milk. They grow and change.

How a Dog Grows

just born   4 weeks old   8 weeks old

How a Duck Grows

just hatched   I week old   3 weeks old

B 22

Ducks **hatch**, or break out of eggs.
Right away ducks can see and move.
They eat seeds. They grow and change.

▷ **How did the dog and duck change?**

12 weeks old   adult

6 weeks old   adult

How does a frog grow and change?

Frogs lay eggs in water. Their young hatch from the eggs. Young frogs are called **tadpoles**. Tadpoles breathe with gills. They have tails to swim. They eat and grow.

How a Frog Grows

eggs

tadpole

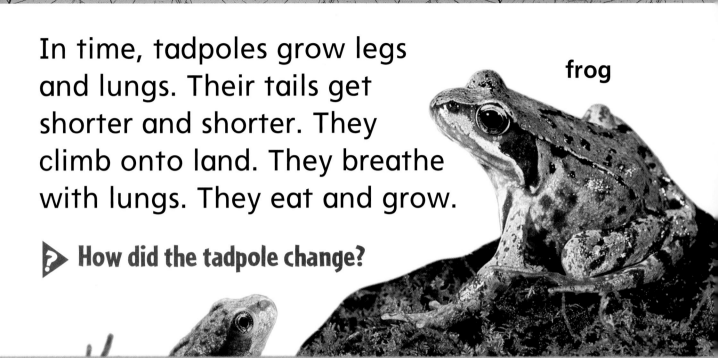

In time, tadpoles grow legs and lungs. Their tails get shorter and shorter. They climb onto land. They breathe with lungs. They eat and grow.

frog

▷ **How did the tadpole change?**

Stop and Think

1. How are dogs, ducks, and frogs alike?
2. How are dogs, ducks, and frogs different?

AT THE COMPUTER Visit **www.mhscience02.com** to learn more about how animals grow and change.

Show How You Grow

Like all animals, people grow and change. As people grow, their looks change.

As people grow, they do different things.

Try This!

Bring in or draw pictures of you as a baby. How have you grown and changed? Talk or write about it.

Draw a Shelter

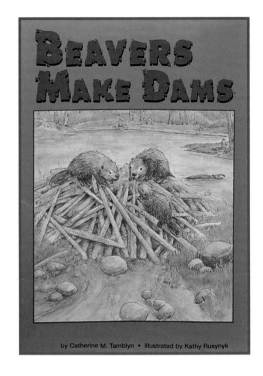

by Catherine M. Tamblyn • illustrated by Kathy Rusynyk

Find out what beavers build. Read *Beavers Make Dams* by Catherine M. Tamblyn.

Try This!

Think about a shelter for you.

- What would it look like?
- Where would you build it?
- What would you use to build it?

Draw a picture. Talk about how the shelter keeps you safe and warm.

Chapter 3 Review

Vocabulary

amphibian

insect

lungs

mammal

gills

tadpole

Use each word once for items 1–6.
What does each picture show?

1

2

3

4

What body part does each animal
use to breathe?

5

6

Science Ideas

7 What are the
kittens doing?

B 28

8 Why do animals move?

9 What are ways in which young animals grow and change?

Science Skill: Classify

10 Tell where each animal goes on the chart.

turtle

duck

bee

fox

frog

goldfish

Group	Name of Animals
Bird	
Insect	
Amphibian	
Reptile	
Fish	
Mammal	

How Animals Meet Their Needs

Vocabulary

food chain
desert
grassland
forest
ocean
pond

Did You Ever Wonder?

How can a little ant carry a big leaf? Many ants work together. They cut up the leaf and bring it home to eat. How else do ants meet their needs?

5 Getting Food

heron

Get Ready

The dragonfly eats an insect.
The frog eats the dragonfly.
What eats the frog?

dragonfly

frog

Science Skill

You put things **in order** when you tell what happens first, next, and last.

Explore Activity

What do some animals eat?

What to do

1 Look at each group of Picture Cards. For each group, think about who eats whom.

2 Put each group of cards **in order**. Start with the animal that is eaten first.

3 For each group, tell who eats whom in order.

What do animals eat?

Some animals eat plants. Some eat other animals. And some eat both.

plant

grasshopper

mouse

A **food chain** shows what animals eat.
First, the grasshopper eats the plants.
Next, the mouse eats the grasshopper.
Last, the coyote eats the mouse.

▶ **What do these animals eat?**

coyote

What helps animals get food?

Animals use their body parts to get food. Some use jaws. Some use sharp teeth and claws. Some use long tongues.

turtle

tiger

anteater

The shape of a bird's beak helps it get food. Some beaks crack seeds open. Some catch fish. And some pick fruit.

grosbeak   heron   toucan

▷ **Which body parts do these animals use to get food?**

Stop and Think

1. What is a food chain?
2. What helps animals get food?

AT THE COMPUTER   Visit **www.mhscience02.com** to find out more about animals.

LESSON 6

Where Animals Live

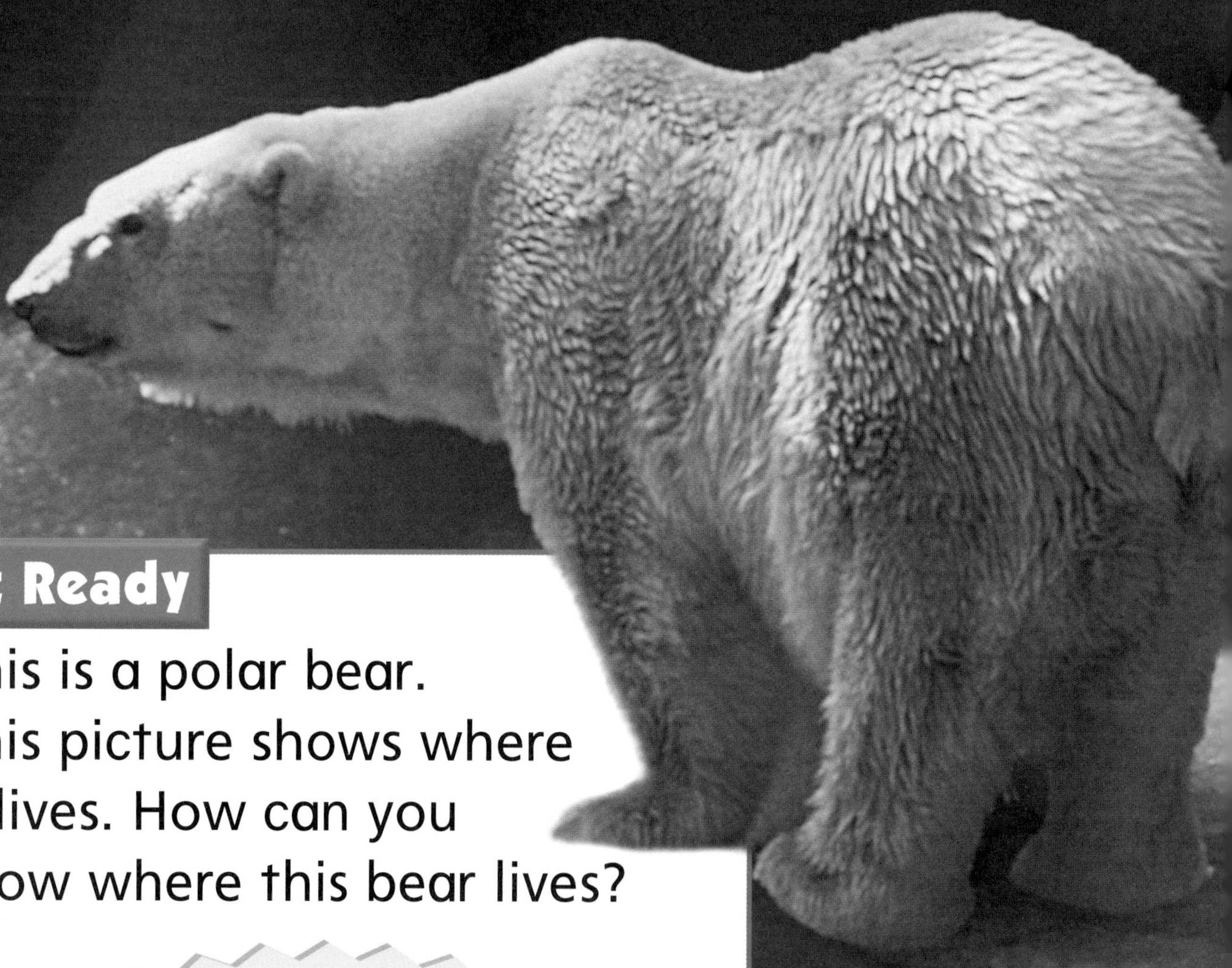

Get Ready

This is a polar bear.
This picture shows where it lives. How can you show where this bear lives?

Science Skill

You can make a model to show how something looks.

Explore Activity

Where does a polar bear live?

What you need

shoebox

paper

cotton

glue

crayons

scissors

What to do

1 Draw a picture of a polar bear. Glue it in your box.

2 Glue cotton in your box for snow.

3 What does your **model** show about where a polar bear lives?

BE CAREFUL!
Scissors are sharp!

Where do land animals live?

Animals live wherever they can find food, water, and shelter.

A **desert** is a place that gets very little rain. Many desert animals get water from the foods they eat.

desert

lizard

horses

grassland

A **grassland** is a place with many grasses. Many animals eat the grasses that grow there.

A **forest** has many trees and other plants. Some animals use the trees for shelter.

owl

▷ **Why can these animals live here?**

forest

Where do water animals live?

An **ocean** is very big and has salt water. Ocean animals get food there.

jellyfish

ocean

pond

crayfish

> **What do these animals get from where they live?**

A **pond** is small and has fresh water. Fresh water has very little salt in it. Many animals find food and stay safe at the pond.

Stop and Think

1. What do animals get from the places where they live?

2. Name two places where land animals live. Name two places where water animals live.

HOME ACTIVITY

Talk about your neighborhood. What animals live there?

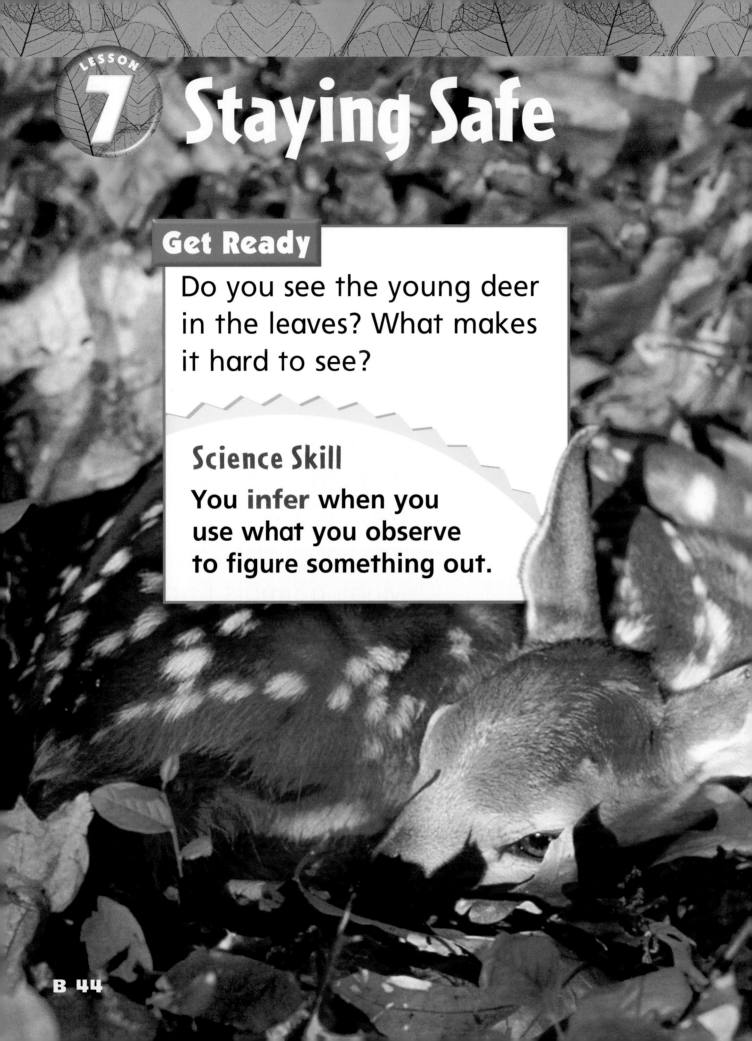

Staying Safe

Get Ready

Do you see the young deer in the leaves? What makes it hard to see?

Science Skill

You **infer** when you use what you observe to figure something out.

Explore Activity

What can make animals hard to see?

newspaper
with
paper fish

What to do

1. Look at the newspaper for one minute. Which fish do you see?

2. Count each kind of fish. Record how many you saw.

3. Which fish were easy to see? Why? **Infer** what made some fish hard to see.

How can color help animals stay safe?

Color helps some animals blend with the land around them. In summer this fox has dark fur. But in winter the fur is white. White fur makes it hard for hungry animals to see the fox in the snow.

summer color

winter color

▶ **How does color help the chameleon stay safe?**

chameleon

How can shape help animals stay safe?

Shape helps some animals stay safe. This insect and fish look like plant parts. Hungry animals can not find them on the plants.

walking stick

▷ **Tell how each animal's shape helps it stay safe.**

sea dragon

What other ways do animals stay safe?

Some animals run to stay safe. This deer leaps to get away. Other animals hide to stay safe. The prairie dog hides in its hole.

deer

Some animals have other ways to stay safe.

armadillo

armadillo staying safe

prairie dog

▷ **How do you think this animal stays safe?**

Stop and Think

1. Tell how color and shape help some animals stay safe.

2. Tell how some animals move or hide to stay safe.

HOME ACTIVITY

Act out ways some animals move to stay safe.

Cave Paintings

Long ago, people drew pictures of animals. They drew them on the walls of caves. We learn about life long ago from these pictures.

Try This!

Make a "cave painting." Draw a picture of an animal that lives today. Draw how people use it.

Make a Graph

José finds out about animals in his yard. He finds them. He counts them. He makes a graph. How many of each animal did José find? Did he find more insects or birds?

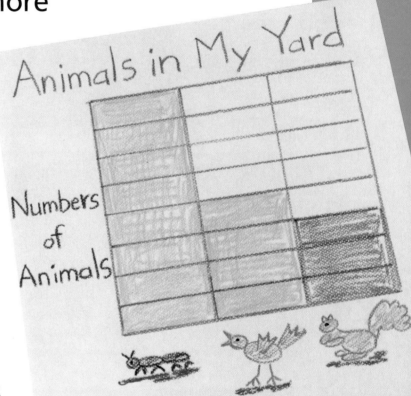

Animals in My Yard

Numbers of Animals

Try This!

How many animals are in your yard or park? Make a graph like this one.

Science Newsroom CD-ROM Choose **Don't Be Dinner** to learn more about animals.

Vocabulary

desert

pond

ocean

forest

food chain

grassland

Use each word once for items 1–6.
What does each picture show?

1

2

3

4

5

6

Science Ideas

How do these animals stay safe?

9 Tell who eats whom.

Science Skill: Communicate

10 How does the beak help this bird? Write or tell about it.

READ
Now You See It, Now You Don't by Geof Smith
Our Busy Tree by K. V. Kudlinski

Susan Hendrickson

FOSSIL HUNTER

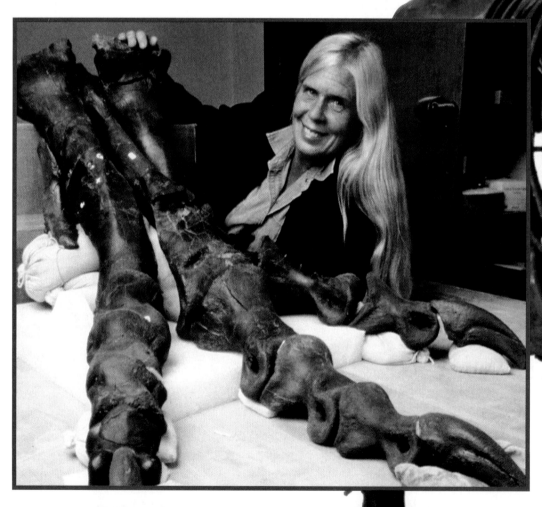

 What does Susan Hendrickson do?

The T. rex
named Sue

Susan Hendrickson hunts for fossils. A fossil may be a bone. It may be a print of a leaf in rock. A fossil is what is left of a living thing from long ago. We learn what life was like long ago by looking at fossils.

One day, Susan found some bones. The bones fit together. They made a big dinosaur. The dinosaur was named Sue.

AT THE COMPUTER

Visit **www.mhscience02.com**
to find out more about fossil hunters.

SCIENCE
Workshop

1. **Draw an animal** you learned about. Be sure your picture answers these questions:

- What does your animal need to live?

- What animal group does it belong to? Label it.

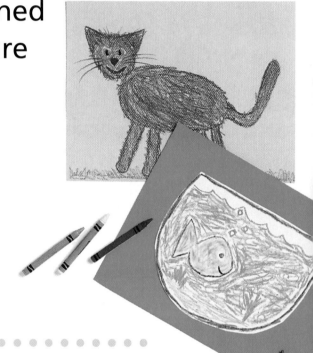

2. **Make a model** of one place where animals live. Make sure your model shows these things:

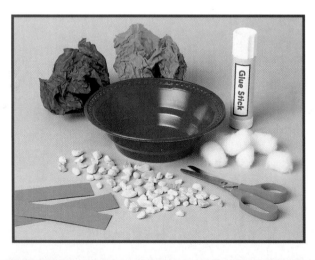

- what kinds of animals live there

- what the animals eat and drink

- where the animals can find shelter

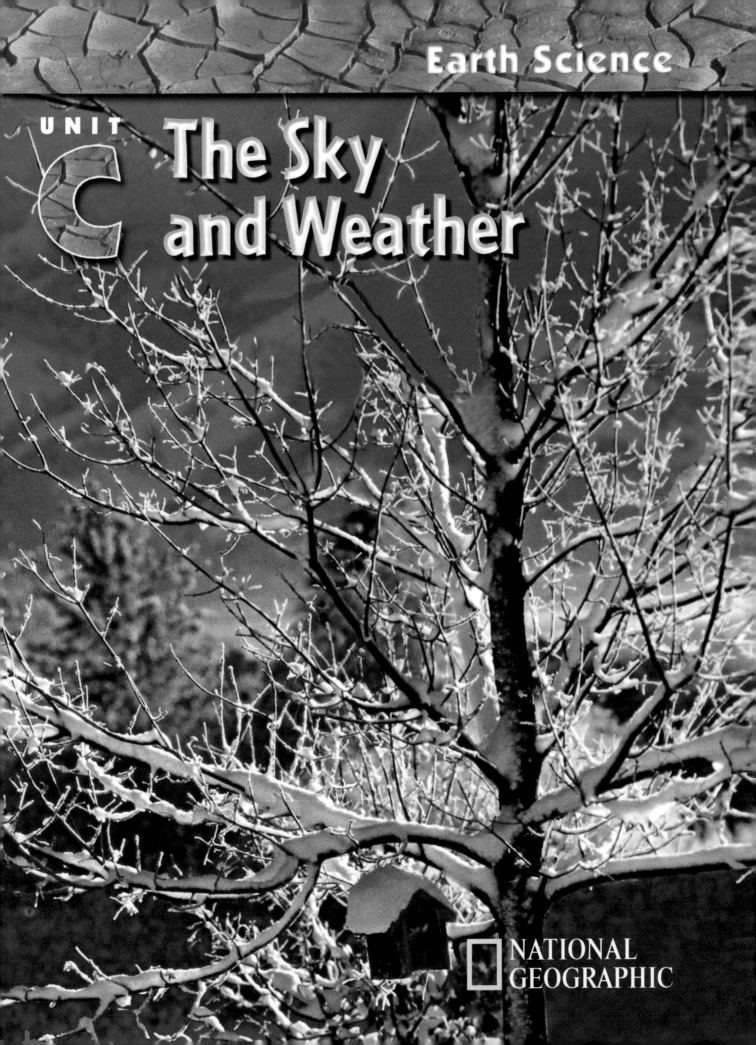

Earth Science

UNIT C

The Sky and Weather

NATIONAL GEOGRAPHIC

The Sky and Weather

LOOK!

What covers the trees and
the ground here? Where do
you think it came from?

The Sky

Did You Ever Wonder?

Where does the Sun go at night? The Sun seems to disappear at night. But it does not. You just can not see it. Where is the Sun in the morning?

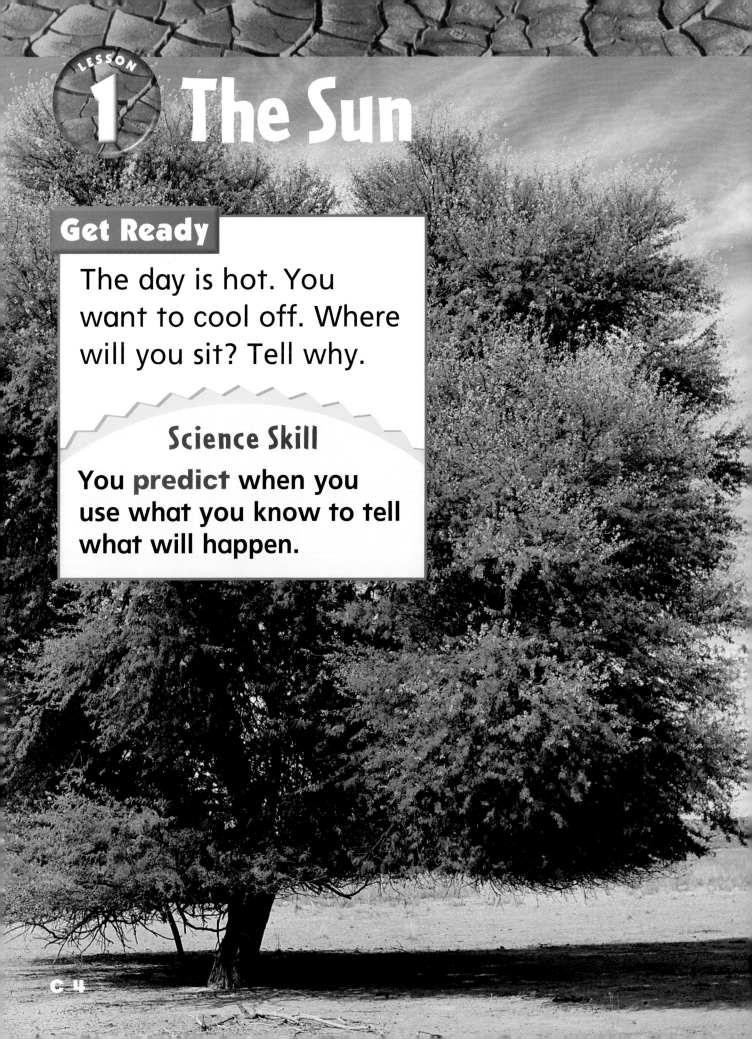

Get Ready

The day is hot. You want to cool off. Where will you sit? Tell why.

Science Skill

You **predict** when you use what you know to tell what will happen.

Explore Activity

2
thermometers

Where will it be warmer?

What to do

1 Will it be warmer in the Sun or in the shade? Tell what you **predict**.

2 Put one thermometer in a sunny place. Put the other in shade. Wait a few minutes.

3 Compare the thermometers. Where is it warmer? Why do you think so? Did you predict this?

sunlight

shade

What does the Sun do?

The Sun is a **star**. Stars glow. They make their own light and heat. The Sun is the star closest to Earth. It is the only star you see during the day.

The Sun lights and heats Earth. Its heat warms Earth's land, water, and air.

You can measure how much the Sun heats things on Earth. **Temperature** is how warm or cool something is.

▷ **What does the Sun do here?**

What can you observe about the Sun?

The Sun seems to move through the sky each day. But the Sun does not really move. Our Earth moves and turns. Each time Earth turns, we have one day and one night.

Morning
When the Sun rises, it looks low in the sky. All morning the Sun gets higher. It warms Earth.

Noon

At noon, the Sun looks high in the sky. On most days, it is warmer than morning. After noon, the Sun gets lower in the sky.

▷ **Tell how the Sun moves through the sky each day.**

Evening

When the Sun sets, it looks low in the sky. The air starts to cool. Soon it is night.

Stop and Think

1. What does Earth get from the Sun?
2. Why do we have day and night?

HOME ACTIVITY Draw what you like to do at different times of day.

The Moon and Stars

Get Ready

The Sun has set. It is night. What do you see in the night sky?

Science Skill

You **observe** when you use your senses to find out about things.

Explore Activity

What can you see in the dark?

shoebox

What to do

1 Make the room dark. Put the glowstick in the box. Cover the box. Look in the end hole. What do you **observe**?

ball

2 Take out the glowstick. Put the ball in the box. Cover it. What do you observe in the box?

glowstick

3 Now shine the flashlight in the side hole. What do you observe? Which things could you see? Why?

flashlight

What can you observe about the Moon?

You can see the Moon on many nights. But the Moon does not make its own light. The Sun lights the Moon.

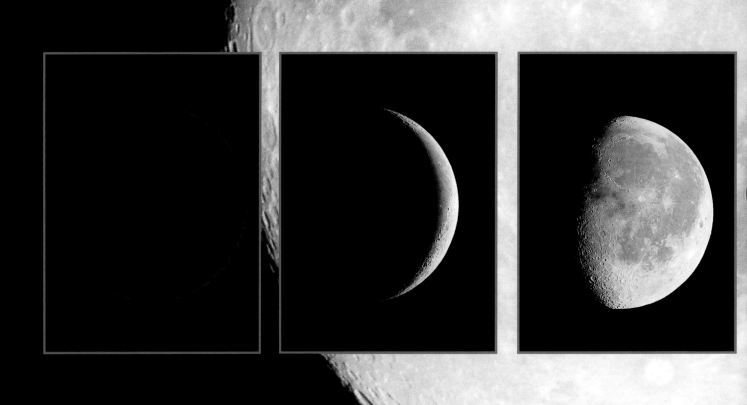

The Moon's shape seems to change each night. But the Moon does not really change shape.

▷ **Tell how the Moon's shape seems to change here.**

What can you observe about the stars?

You can see the stars glow at night. Stars make their own light and heat. But you can not feel their heat. They are too far away.

Big Dipper

Little Dipper

Groups of stars seem to make pictures in the sky. A star picture is called a **constellation**. Constellations can look like people, animals, or things.

> **What does the Big Dipper constellation look like?**

Stop and Think

1. Why can we see the Moon at night?
2. What is a constellation?

MORE TO READ Read **Moondance** by Frank Asch.

The Planets

LESSON 3

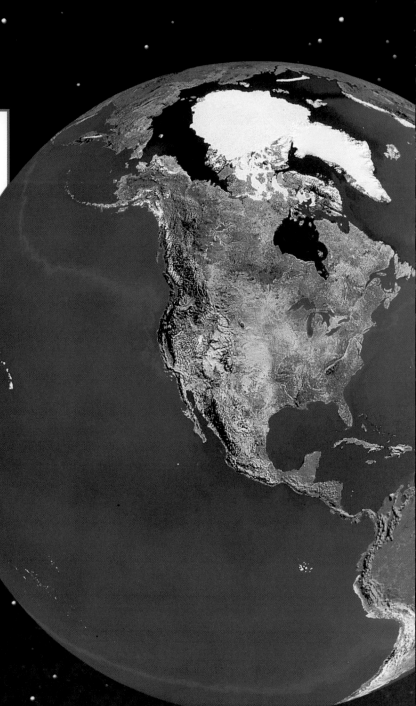

This is Earth. Earth moves. How can you show how Earth moves?

Science Skill

You can **make a model** to show how something moves.

Explore Activity

How does Earth move around the Sun?

What you need

Earth label

Sun

Sun label

string

What to do

1 Make labels for "Earth" and "Sun." You be the "Earth." Let a partner be the "Sun."

2 **Make a model** to show how Earth moves around the Sun. Have the "Sun" stand still. Walk around the "Sun" a few times.

3 Trade labels. Let the "Earth" walk around you. How does Earth move around the Sun? Talk about it.

What are the planets?

Earth is a **planet**. It moves around the Sun. There are other planets, too.

Mercury

Venus

Earth

Mars

Jupiter

Earth

Some planets are big. Some are small. Some are very close to the Sun. Others are very far away from it.

But big or small, near or far, all planets move around the Sun.

 **How are the planets alike?**

Uranus

Neptune

Pluto

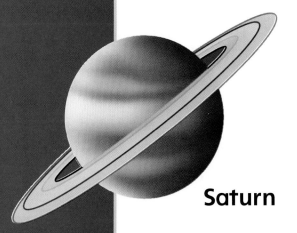

Saturn

Stop and Think

1. Does Earth stay in one place? Tell about it.

2. How are all planets alike? How are they different?

 **AT THE COMPUTER** Visit **www.mhscience02.com** to find out more about the planets.

Moon Stories

Long ago, people near and far made up stories. Some were about the Moon. Some stories told about things that lived there. Others told about what made the Moon's many shapes.

Try This!

Make up your own story about the Moon. Make drawings to go with it.

Make a Star Picture

You can see many star pictures in the night sky. You may see one that no one has before!

Try This!

Draw a small picture on some foil. Poke tiny holes along the picture. Put the foil on a paper towel roll. Look into it. What do you see?

Science Newsroom CD-ROM
Choose **Constellations** to learn more about stars.

C 21

Vocabulary

temperature

constellation

planet

star

Use each word once for items 1–4. What does each picture show?

1

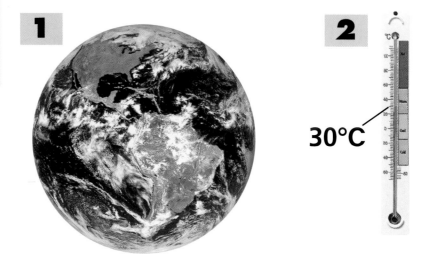

2

30°C

3

4

Science Ideas

5 What does Earth get from the Sun?

6 Why can you see the Moon at night?

7 How are the planets alike?

Science Skill: Observe

Does each picture show morning or noon?
Tell why you think so.

READ
Under the Night Sky by Linda Ross

CHAPTER 6

Weather and Seasons

Vocabulary

weather

wind

clouds

season

spring

summer

fall

winter

Did You Ever Wonder?

Why are rain clouds so dark? They are dark because they hold a lot of water. What will happen to the water?

LESSON 4 Weather

How do you think the air feels here? Tell about it.

Science Skill

You **observe** when you use your senses to find out about things.

Explore Activity

What can you observe about the air?

What to do

1. Make the weather tool below.

2. Take both weather tools outside. **Observe** each one for a few minutes.

3. Go other places outside the school. Observe each tool for a few minutes. What did you observe about the air in different places?

craft stick

streamer

tape

thermometer

What is weather?

Weather is what the air is like outside. The air may be warm or cool. The air may be moving. The air may not be moving at all. Moving air is called **wind**.

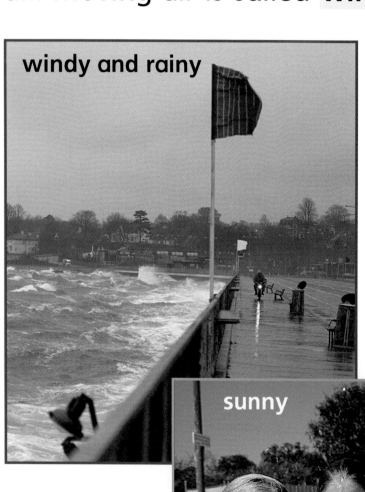

windy and rainy

sunny

The sky may be sunny and clear. It may be cloudy. It may even rain or snow.

foggy

snowy

▷ Tell about the weather here.

What makes it rain or snow?

Rain or snow falls from **clouds**. Clouds are made from lots of tiny water drops that are in the air.

1 Water goes into the air. You can't see this water.

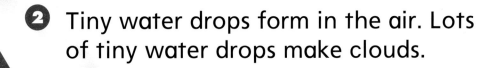

2 Tiny water drops form in the air. Lots of tiny water drops make clouds.

3 The water drops in clouds get bigger. When the water drops get big enough, they fall as rain or snow.

▷ **What happens when water drops in clouds get very big?**

Stop and Think

1. What is weather?

2. How are rain and snow made?

HOME ACTIVITY

Draw a picture of a rainy day.

Get Ready

Before, it was sunny. But the weather changed. What is the weather like now?

Science Skill

You **communicate** when you make a chart to tell facts.

Explore Activity

How does the weather change in a week?

What to do

1 Use your chart and weather tools. Observe the weather for one week.

2 Fill in the chart each day.

3 How did the weather change? How does your chart **communicate** this?

weather chart

thermometer

weather tool

	Monday	Tuesday	Wednesday	Thursday	Friday
☀	✓				
🌡	✓				
☁					
🌧					
❄					
🌡	cool				

When does the weather change?

The weather changes when the air outside changes. It may be rainy and cloudy. Then the rain stops. The clouds go away. Soon, it is sunny.

a sunny day after rainfall

Sun, rain, and wind can help things live and grow. But some weather is dangerous. It can harm living things. It can harm the land, too.

▶ **Tell about the weather here.**

tornado

hurricane

drought

How do we measure weather?

People use many tools
to measure weather.

An anemometer
tells how fast the
wind blows.

A wind sock shows the
direction of the wind.

A thermometer
tells how warm
or cool the air is.

▷ **What do these tools measure?**

A meteorologist uses tools to measure weather.

A rain gauge tells how much rain falls.

Stop and Think

1. When can weather change?

2. What are some things that weather tools measure?

MORE TO READ   Read **The Big Storm** by Bruce Hiscock.

C 37

Spring and Summer

Get Ready

What are these children doing? What is the weather like here?

Science Skill

You **communicate** when you talk, draw, or write to share ideas.

Explore Activity

Is the weather the same all year?

drawing
paper

crayons

What to do

1 Draw yourself when it is very warm outside. Draw the weather. Draw what you wear.

2 Draw yourself when it is very cold outside. Draw the weather. Draw what you wear.

3 Is the weather the same all year? Do you wear the same kinds of clothes all year? **Communicate** your ideas.

What happens in spring?

A **season** is a time of the year. **Spring** is the season after winter. It is warmer in spring than in winter. In some places, it may rain a lot. In spring, the days get longer and the nights get shorter.

In spring, birds build nests and lay eggs. Other animals have their young, too.

Plants grow new leaves and flowers. Many people plant seeds. Rain and warmth help the seeds grow.

▶ What do living things do in spring?

What happens in summer?

Summer is the season after spring. It is warmer in summer than in spring. In some places, it may be very hot. Summer days are longer than the nights.

The warmth and longer daylight hours help plants grow. Many plants grow flowers, seeds, and fruits.

Young animals grow bigger and look more like their parents. Many people spend more time outside in summer.

 **What do living things do in summer?**

Stop and Think

1. What are spring and summer like?

2. What are some things living things do in spring?

AT THE COMPUTER

Visit **www.mhscience02.com** to learn more about the seasons.

Get Ready

What is the season here?
How do you know?

Science Skill

You **observe** when you
use your senses to find
out about things.

Explore Activity

How can you stay warm when it is cold outside?

What to do

1 Pick up the cup. Hold it in your hand. **Observe** how it feels.

2 Wait a few minutes. Put on the glove. Hold the cup again in your hand. Observe how it feels.

3 When did your hand feel less cold? How can you stay warm when it is cold outside?

What happens in fall?

Fall is the season after summer. It is cooler in fall than in summer. The days get shorter and the nights get longer.

Many plants stop growing in fall. In some places, leaves change color and drop to the ground. In many places, fruits are ripe. People pick the fruits.

Some animals move to warmer places in fall. Others store food to eat in winter.

▷ **What do living things do in fall?**

What happens in winter?

Winter is the season after fall. It is colder in winter than in fall. In some places, it may be very cold. People wear warm clothes. Winter days are shorter than the nights.

In many places, some plants die. Some stay alive but have no leaves. Evergreens make food all year.

Where winter is cold, there is not much food for animals. Some eat what they can find. Some eat what they store. And some go to sleep until spring.

▶ **What do living things do in winter?**

Stop and Think

1. What do some living things do in fall?

2. What is winter like?

AT THE COMPUTER

Visit **www.mhscience02.com** to learn more about the seasons.

Busy Seasons

Find out about some things people do in fall. Read *Fall is Fun* by Joe Smith.

by Joe Smith
illustrated by Selina Alko

Try This!

Make your own book. Call it *Winter Is Fun*. Show things that people do in winter.

Measure Temperature

What is the temperature like in a season? Does it change a lot from day to day? Find out.

Try This!

Work with an adult. Find out the temperature each day. Use a radio, a TV, or a thermometer. Do it at the same time each day. Do it for a few weeks. Record the temperatures. What are they like?

Vocabulary

weather

wind

season

spring

summer

fall

winter

clouds

Use each word once for items 1–8. What does each picture show?

Complete each sentence.

6 A time of year is called a ____.

7 Moving air is called ____.

8 What the air is like outside is called ____.

Science Ideas

Tell what each weather tool measures.

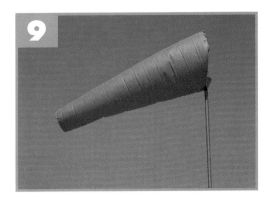

9

10

Science Skill: Communicate

11 What makes it rain or snow?
Use the picture to tell what happens.

READ
Fall Is Fun! by Joe Smith

Warren Faidley
Storm Chaser

Warren Faidley is a storm chaser.
He looks for tornadoes.

Tornadoes happen in some thunderstorms. Warren drives to where these thunderstorms are forming. He watches the clouds. If Warren sees a tornado, he tells others where it is. He also tells where the storm may be going. This information can save lives.

 How does Warren Faidley help save lives?

 Visit **www.mhscience02.com** to find out more about storm chasers.

SCIENCE
Workshop

1. Tell about things in the sky. Draw your school. Show the Sun. Draw your house. Show the Moon and stars. Then write an answer for each question below.

- What happens each time the Earth turns?

- What lights the Moon?

- What is a constellation?

2. Compare winter and summer where you live. Draw pictures of what you do and wear in summer and winter. Then write a sentence about:

- the weather in summer

- the weather in winter

UNIT D

Caring for Earth

NATIONAL GEOGRAPHIC

Caring for Earth

LOOK!

People planted these trees. Why do people plant trees? What can people get from them?

7

Earth's Resources

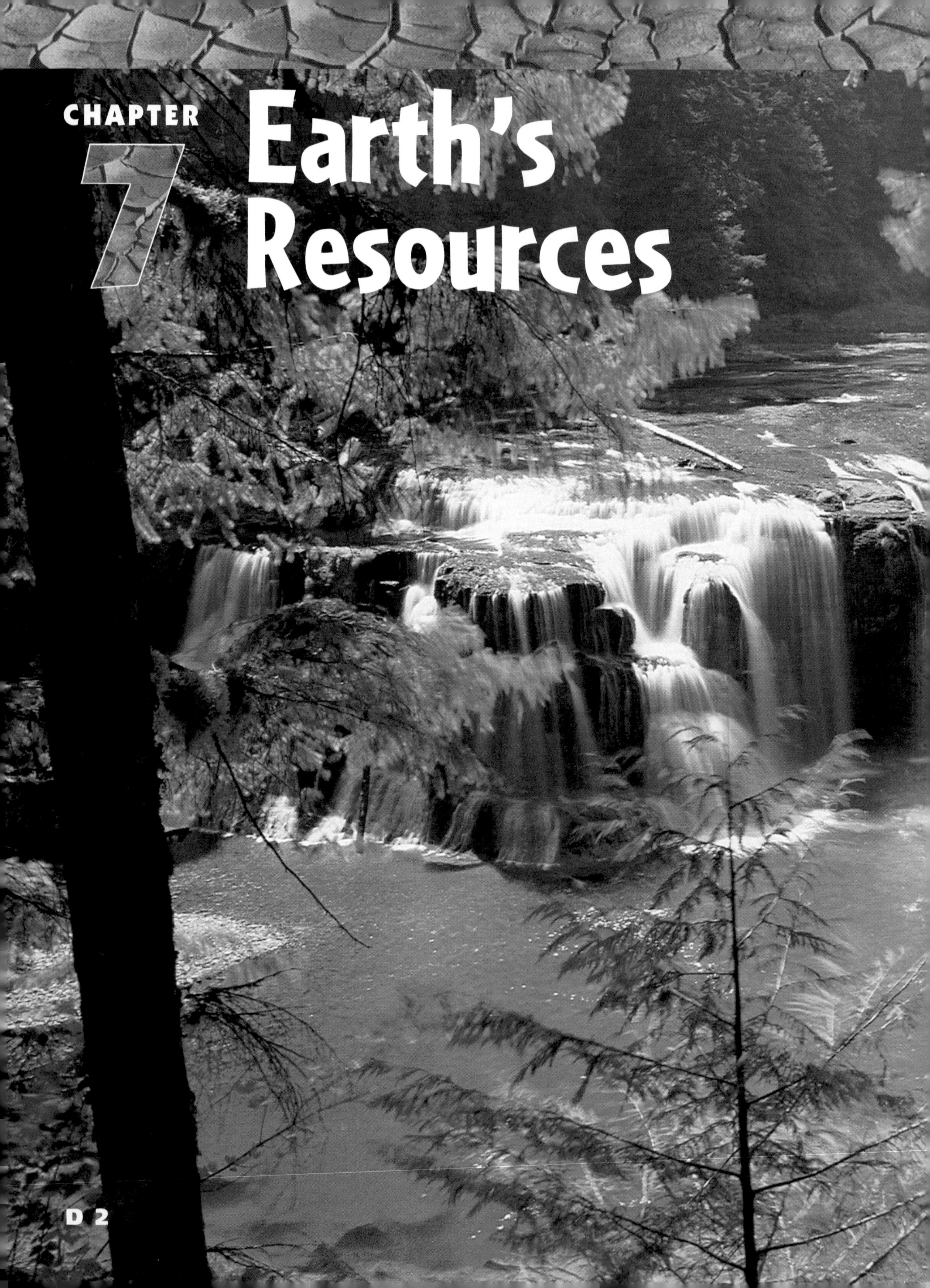

Vocabulary

rocks

minerals

natural resource

soil

oxygen

Did You Ever Wonder?

Where does water come from? Water falls to Earth as snow or rain. It flows into streams and rivers. Then it collects in ponds, lakes, and oceans. Why is water important?

Rocks and Minerals

Get Ready

Did you ever collect rocks? How can the rocks be put into groups?

Science Skill

You **classify** when you group things by how they are alike.

Explore Activity

How can you classify rocks?

1 Look at each rock with the hand lens. Feel each rock.

2 Draw two sorting rings. **Classify** the rocks. Label the groups you make.

3 How did you classify the rocks?

What you need

rocks

hand lens

paper

What are rocks and minerals?

Rocks are nonliving things from Earth. The land we live on is mostly rock.

Minerals are the building blocks of rock. They give rocks their color. Some rocks are made of many minerals. Other rocks are made of only one mineral.

mineral

Rocks may be big or small. They may be smooth or rough. They may be different colors, too.

▶ **Tell how these rocks are alike and different.**

Why are rocks and minerals important?

A rock is a natural resource. So is a mineral. So is land. A **natural resource** is something from Earth that people use.

We use rocks to build things. We use minerals to make glass, jewelry, and metals.

▷ **How are rocks and minerals used here?**

Stop and Think

1. What is a natural resource?

2. How do people use rocks and minerals?

HOME ACTIVITY

Which rocks and minerals do you use at home?

Soil

Get Ready

The machine digs into the ground. It pulls up soil. Does all this soil look the same?

Science Skill

You **compare**, when you learn how things are alike and different.

Explore Activity

How do some soils compare?

1. Use a hand lens. **Compare** each soil. How does each soil look and smell?

2. Squeeze each soil with your hand. What happens to each soil? Wash your hands.

3. What is different about each soil?

3 plates of different soils

hand lens

topsoil

sandy soil

clay soil

What is soil?

Soil is made of tiny bits of rock. It may also have bits of dead animals and plants in it. There is also air and water in soil.

In most places, soil covers the land. Soils can be very different.

Topsoil is dark brown or black. It sticks together when you squeeze it. It holds some water. Plants grow best in topsoil.

Clay soil may be brown, red, or yellow. It sticks together when you squeeze it. It holds a lot of water.

Sandy soil may be light brown. It does not stick together when you squeeze it. It does not hold much water.

▷ **Tell about each of these soils.**

Why is soil important?

Soil is a natural resource. People use it to make things like bricks and clay pots.

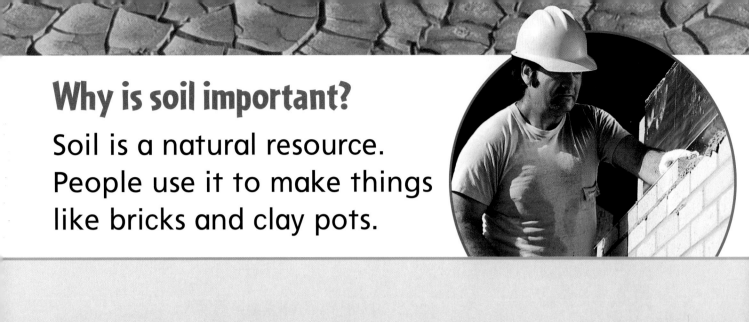

People grow plants in soil. People and animals eat these plants. Soil is also the home for many animals.

▷ **How is soil used here?**

Stop and Think

1. What is soil made of?
2. Why is soil important?

AT THE COMPUTER

Visit **www.mhscience02.com** to learn more about soil.

Get Ready

It rains in the mountains. The water forms a stream. Where does it go?

Science Skill

You **communicate** when you talk, write, or draw.

Explore Activity

What happens to rain?

sand

water

deep tray

1 Use the sand to make a mountain.

2 Pour water on the model mountain. Pour it at the top of the mountain. Wash your hands.

3 What happens to the water? **Communicate** your ideas.

Where is Earth's water found?

Most of Earth has water on it. Rain falls from clouds. It flows from the land into streams, rivers, and lakes. There is fresh water in clouds, streams, rivers, and lakes. Fresh water is the kind of water you drink.

river

Most of Earth's water is in oceans. Ocean water is salt water. People can not drink salt water. But many plants and animals live in salt water.

 Where is Earth's fresh water found?

Most of Earth is covered with water.

lake

ocean

Why is water important?

Water is a natural resource. All living things need water.

People use water to drink, to cook, and to clean. People travel across water. People use water to have fun, too.

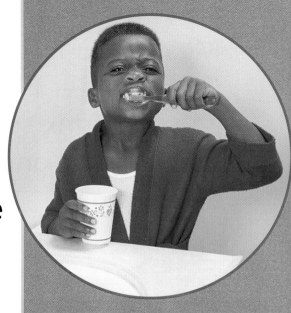

People use moving water to make power. The power lights and heats their homes.

▷ **How is water used here?**

Stop and Think

1. Where is most of Earth's water?

2. How do people use water?

HOME ACTIVITY How do you use water to have fun? Make a drawing.

LESSON 4 Air

Get Ready

What makes the balloon move across the sky?

Science Skill

You **infer** when you use what you know to figure something out.

Explore Activity

balloon

What can make the balloon move?

1 Tape a finish line to the floor.

2 Use the straw. Move the balloon to the finish line. Do not touch the balloon with the straw.

drinking straw

3 **Infer** what makes the balloon move. How could you move it faster with the straw? Try it.

tape

Why is air important?

Air is a natural resource. Air fills basketballs. People fly planes in the air. They use air to move sailboats and make music. Moving air can even make power for homes.

People take in air. Air has **oxygen** in it. Oxygen is a part of air that people need to live.

▶ **How is air used here?**

Stop and Think

1. What are some ways people use air?
2. What is in air that people need?

 **AT THE COMPUTER**

Visit **www.mhscience02.com** to learn more about air.

Living Things Are Resources

Get Ready

Do you eat any of these foods?
Which come from plants?
Which come from animals?

Science Skill

You **classify** when you group things by where they come from.

Explore Activity

What comes from plants and animals?

What you need

sticky notes

crayons

1 Write the word *plant* on some sticky notes. Write the word *animal* on other sticky notes.

2 Go around the classroom. **Classify** where some things come from. Put sticky notes on them.

3 Talk about the things you classified.

Why are plants important?

Plants are a natural resource. People eat plants. They use plants for food. People also use wood from trees to make many things.

wheat bread

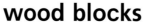

wood blocks

Cotton comes from plants. People use cotton to make many things.

Plants make oxygen. People need oxygen to live.

cotton towels

▷ **How are plants used here?**

maple syrup

Why are animals important?

Animals are a natural resource. Many people eat meat from animals. Milk and eggs come from them, too. Some wool comes from sheep. Things made from wool keep people warm.

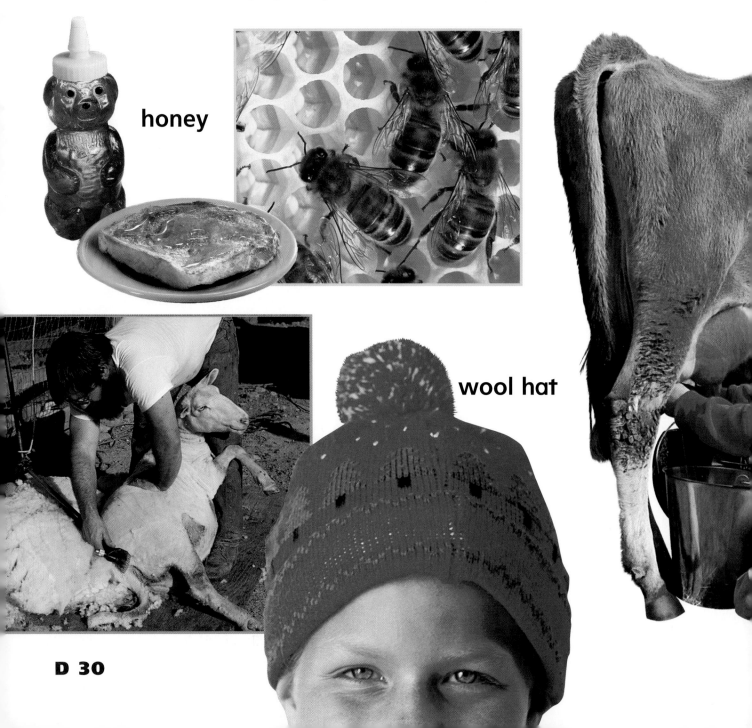

honey

wool hat

Many people have animals as pets. Some animals help people get from place to place.

How are animals used here?

milk

Stop and Think

1. What are two ways people use plants?

2. What are two ways people use animals?

MORE TO READ

Read **The Great Kapok Tree** by Lynne Cherry.

Getting Water

You get water from a sink. But long ago, people did not have water in their homes.

Try This!

Talk with an adult. What would life be like without water in your home? Where would you get water to drink? How would you wash things?

A Poem About Earth

Read this poem with an adult.
It's about Earth's air and land.

I'm glad the sky is painted blue,
And the earth is painted green,
With such a lot of nice fresh air
all sandwiched in between.
—Anonymous

Try This!

Write your own poem about Earth's
air, land, or water. Make drawings to
go with your poem.

Vocabulary

rocks

mineral

soil

natural resource

oxygen

Use each word once for items 1–5. What does each picture show?

1

2

3

4

5

Science Ideas

6 Tell how these soils are alike and different.

clay soil

topsoil

sandy soil

7 Tell where you can find Earth's water.

8 What are some ways people use air?

Tell if each thing comes from plants, animals, or rocks.

9

10

11

12

Taking Care of
Earth

Did You Ever Wonder?

How can we take care of land, water, air, and living things? One way is to make parks. These bears stay safe in their park home. How else can we take care of land, water, air, and living things?

6 Pollution

Get Ready

Do you see the smoke?
Where does it go?

Science Skill

You **observe** when
you use your senses to
find out about things.

Explore Activity

white paper

petroleum jelly

hand lens

What is in the air?

1 Wipe some petroleum jelly on the paper. **Observe** it with the hand lens. Wash your hands.

2 Place the paper outside for a few hours. Put something on the paper to hold it in place.

3 Observe the paper again with the hand lens. What is on the paper? How do you think it got there?

What is pollution?

Harmful things in the air, water, or land are called **pollution**. Pollution happens when air, water, or land gets dirty. It can harm living and nonliving things.

Smoke from factories pollutes the air. So does smoke from cars, planes, and forest fires.

Air pollution may make people sick. They can't breathe the way they should.

 What pollutes the air?

What pollutes the water?

Wastes pollute the water. Wastes are things left over from factories. Dirty water is not safe to drink.

Sometimes people throw trash into water. When animals eat this trash, they may get sick and die.

▷ **What happened to the fish?**

What pollutes the land?

Trash pollutes the land. So do factory wastes. Land pollution may harm animals, plants, and soil. Plants and crops can't grow in polluted soil.

▷ **What pollutes the land here?**

Stop and Think

1. What are three kinds of pollution?

2. How may pollution harm living things?

 **AT THE COMPUTER** Visit **www.mhscience02.com** to learn more about pollution.

Caring for Earth's Resources

Get Ready

Look closely. What is this house made of? How else can people use things to make something new?

Science Skill

You **investigate** when you make a plan and try it out.

Explore Activity

How can you make something new from something old?

1 **Investigate** how you can use clean, old things to make something new. Think about what you want to make.

2 Make a plan. Think about what you will use to make it. Try it out.

3 Tell how you used something old in a new way.

clean, old things

art supplies

Why should people reuse things?

When people **reuse** things, they use them again in a new way. They don't throw these things away. They don't have to buy new things.

▷ **How do people reuse things here?**

Why should people recycle?

When people **recycle**, they help turn old things into new things. Old paper is used to make new paper. This means trees are not cut to make new paper. This saves trees.

▷ **What do these children recycle?**

Why should people reduce what they use?

When people **reduce** what they use, they use less of it. Then there is more left over for later. You can reduce how much paper you use when you write on both sides. This saves paper.

▷ Who uses less paper here? Tell how.

What else can people do?

People can take care of resources in other ways. They take care of air when they drive cars less. They take care of water when they keep it clean. They take care of land when they put trash in cans.

▶ **How do these people take care of resources?**

Stop and Think

1. Why is it important to reuse, recycle, and reduce?

2. How can you help stop pollution and take care of natural resources? Tell one way.

 Read **Recycle!** by Gail Gibbons.

Going for a Walk

written by Kana Riley   illustrated by Margeaux Lucas

A Trip to the Park

Find out some things you can see and do in a park. Read *Going for a Walk* by Kana Riley.

Try This!

How can people keep a park's living things safe? How can people keep a park's land, air, and water clean? Make a picture book to show how. Call the book *Save Our Parks.*

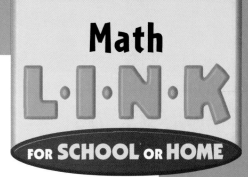

Make Less Trash

Each person in your family makes 4 pounds of trash each day. But only 1 pound of that trash is reused or recycled!

Try This!

How much trash does your family make each day? Add to find out. How much of that trash is reused or recycled? Add to find out.

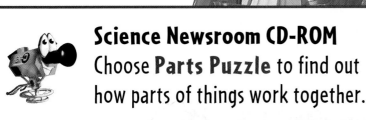

Science Newsroom CD-ROM
Choose **Parts Puzzle** to find out how parts of things work together.

Vocabulary

pollution

reduce

reuse

recycle

Use each word once for items 1–4. What does each picture show?

1

2

3

4

Science Ideas

5 What happens if people don't take care of the air?

6 Name some things that make pollution.

7 Tell one way that people can reuse things.

Science Skill: Observe

8 What natural resources are not taken care of here? How do you know?

READ
In the Lake by Gary Apple
Billy Fish by Edward S. Popper

The Return of the
American Bison

Once there were many American bison. But people hunted bison for food and for their skins. Many people hunted them just for sport. By 1900, very few bison were left.

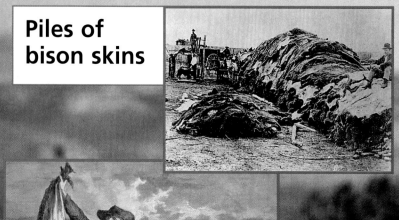

Piles of bison skins

Bison killed for its skin

William Hornaday wanted to help the bison. In 1905, he helped start the American Buffalo Society. (Buffalo is another name for bison.) They worked to bring back bison. Today bison again live in the wild. People still work to save them.

Why did the American bison almost die out?

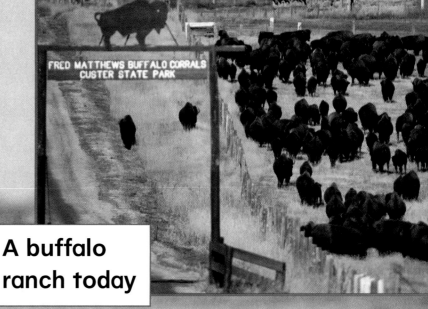

FRED MATTHEWS BUFFALO CORRALS
CUSTER STATE PARK

A buffalo ranch today

AT THE COMPUTER

Visit **www.mhscience02.com** for more amazing stories and facts.

SCIENCE
Workshop

1. **Make a poster.** Think of five natural resources. How do people use them? Use words and pictures to show.

2. **Make a mobile** of drawings. Be sure to show a drawing for each of these:

- air pollution
- land pollution
- water pollution
- something that can be reused
- something that can be recycled

UNIT E

Matter, Matter Everywhere

NATIONAL GEOGRAPHIC

UNIT E Physical Science

Matter, Matter Everywhere

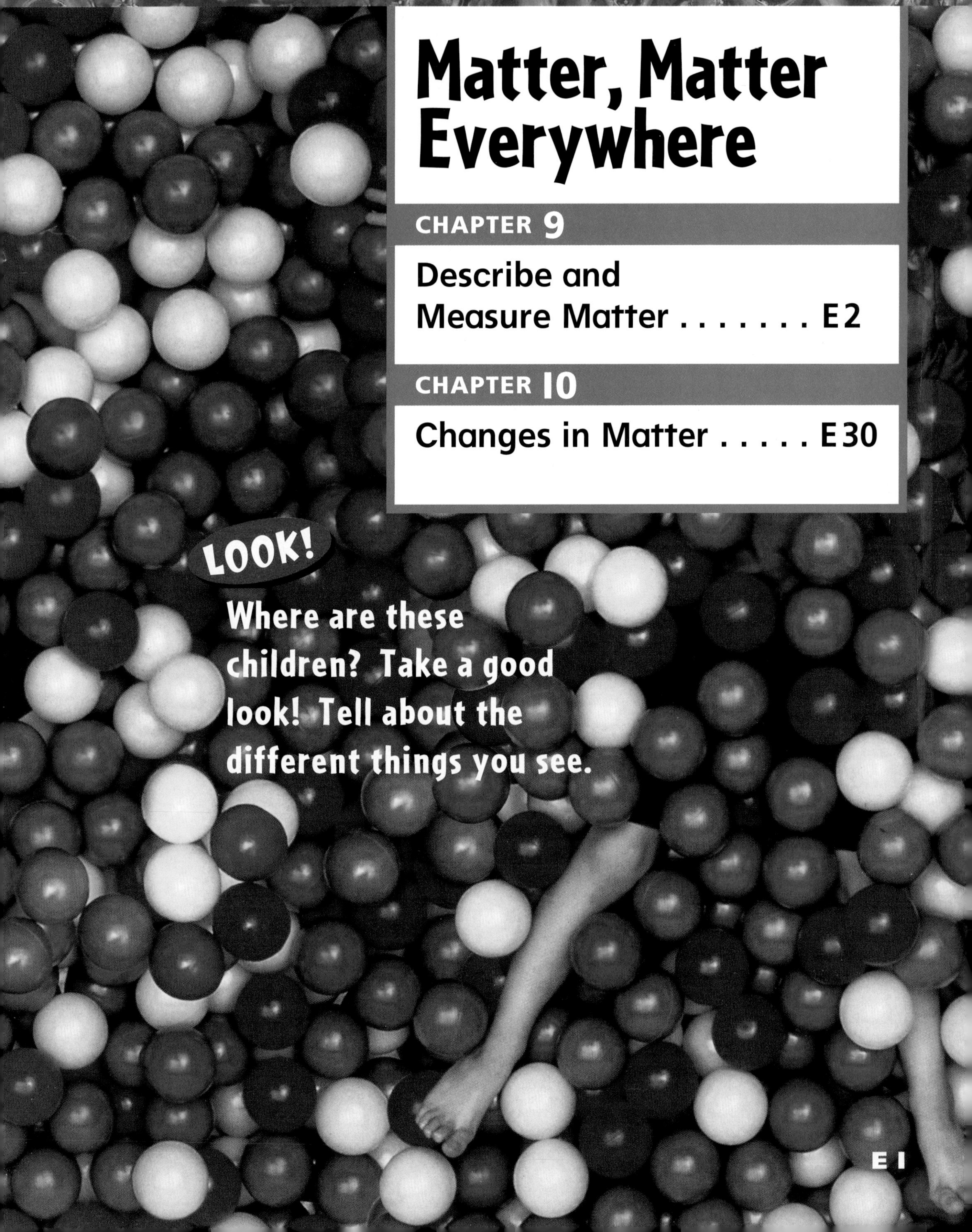

LOOK!

Where are these children? Take a good look! Tell about the different things you see.

Describe and Measure
Matter

Vocabulary

matter
properties
mass
solid
ruler
balance
liquid
measuring cup
gas

Did You Ever Wonder?

What is inside a balloon? Air!
Air gives the balloon its shape.
Would the air stay the same shape
if you let it out of the balloon?

1 Properties of Matter

Get Ready

The boy swims in the wet pool. He breathes the warm air. What else do you observe?

Science Skill

You **observe** when you use your senses to find out about things.

Explore Activity

What do you observe about some things?

balloon

cup of water

spoon

block

What to do

1 Feel the block. What do you **observe**? Drop the block. Talk about its shape.

2 Feel the water. What do you observe? Stir the water. Talk about its shape.

3 Gently squeeze the balloon. What do you think is inside? Talk about what you observe.

What is matter?

Matter is what makes up all things. A boat is made of matter. Clouds are made of matter. Water is made of matter. You are made of matter, too!

Matter is all around you. It can have different shapes or no shape of its own. You can see some matter. Other matter you can not see at all.

▶ **What is matter here?**

What are some properties of matter?

Matter has different **properties**. How something feels, looks, smells, tastes, or sounds are properties. Color, size, and space are some properties.

Some things take up a lot of space. Others take up a little.

The large dog takes up more space than the small dog.

Mass is another property of matter. Mass is how much matter is in an object. Heavier things have more mass than lighter things.

The metal ball has more mass than the basketball.

▷ **Tell about the properties of the objects you see here.**

Stop and Think

1. What is matter?
2. Do big things always have more mass than small things? Tell about it.

The balloon has less mass than the pumpkin.

HOME ACTIVITY Go on a matter hunt. Tell about the matter you find.

Solids

Get Ready

Look at these things. How are they alike? How are they different?

Science Skill

You **compare** when you tell how things are alike and different.

Explore Activity

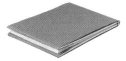

book

pencil

eraser

balance

How does some matter compare?

What to do

1. Use the balance to **compare** these things. Which things have more mass? Which things have less mass?

2. Compare the things in other ways. How do they look? How do they feel?

3. How are the things alike? How are they different?

What are solids?

A **solid** is one kind of matter. A solid has mass and takes up space. Only a solid has a shape of its own. That means a solid keeps its shape even when you move it.

Solids have other properties. Solids may be smooth or rough. They may be soft or hard. They may be different colors, too.

▶ **Talk about the properties of these solids.**

How can you measure solids?

You can use a **ruler** to measure a solid. A ruler measures how long, how tall, or how big around something is.

You can use a **balance** to measure the mass of a solid. The pan with more mass goes down.

What can you find out about the toy car by using the balance?

Stop and Think

1. How are solids alike? How are they different?

2. What can you use to measure solids?

HOME ACTIVITY Use a ruler. Measure long solids. Measure short solids.

Liquids

Get Ready

What happened to the milk?

Science Skill

You **draw a conclusion** when you use what you observe to explain what happened.

Explore Activity

different-
shaped
containers

water

Can water change shape?

What to do

1 Pour some water into one container. Draw the shape of the water.

2 Pour the same water into the other container. Draw the shape of the water.

3 What would the shape of the water be in the third container? Try it.

4 Can you **draw a conclusion** about the shape of water? Talk about it.

What are liquids?

A **liquid** is a kind of
matter. A liquid has mass
and takes up space. It flows when you
pour it. It has no shape of its own. A liquid
takes the shape of what you pour it in.

E 18

water

syrup

Some liquids are thick. They flow slowly.
Others are thin. They flow quickly.
Liquids can also be different colors.

▶ **What are the properties of these liquids?**

How can you measure liquids?

You can use a **measuring cup** to measure a liquid. A measuring cup measures how much space a liquid takes up. Measuring spoons and droppers measure liquids, too.

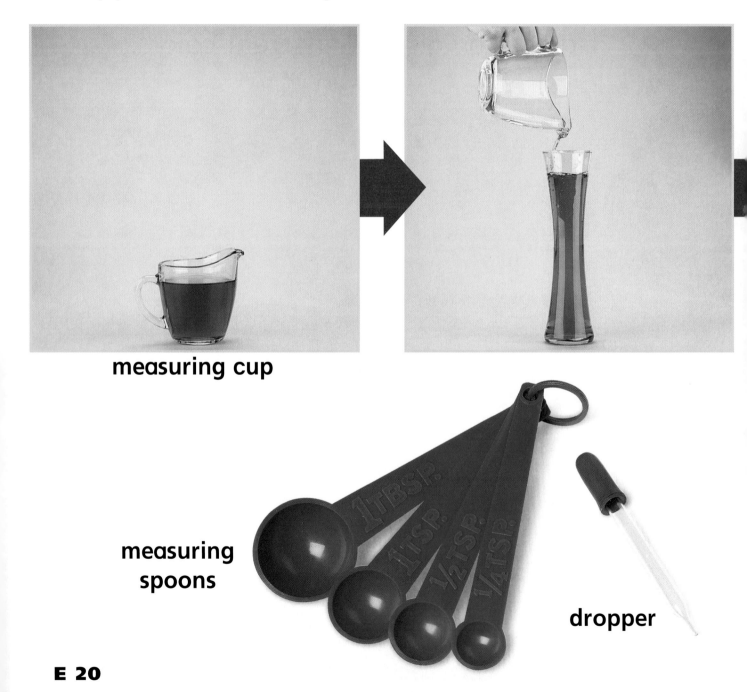

measuring cup

measuring spoons

dropper

These pictures show one cup of liquid in different containers. The liquid's shape looks different in each one. But there is one cup of liquid in each of them.

▷ **What can you find out about a liquid when you put it in a measuring cup?**

Stop and Think

1. How are liquids alike? How are they different?

2. What can you use to measure liquids?

AT THE COMPUTER

Visit **www.mhscience02.com** to find out more about liquids.

Gases

Get Ready

The girl blows bubbles. What is inside each one?

Science Skill

You **infer** when you use what you know to figure something out.

Explore Activity

tissue

plastic cup

What keeps the tissue dry?

What to do

1 Stuff the tissue in the bottom of the cup.

2 Turn the cup upside down. Push the cup down to the bottom of the tray of water.

3 Pull the cup up. Feel the tissue. **Infer** why it stays dry.

pan of water

What are gases?

A **gas** is a kind of matter. A gas has mass and takes up space. Like a liquid, a gas takes the shape of what it is in. But a gas spreads out to fill all the space of what it is in.

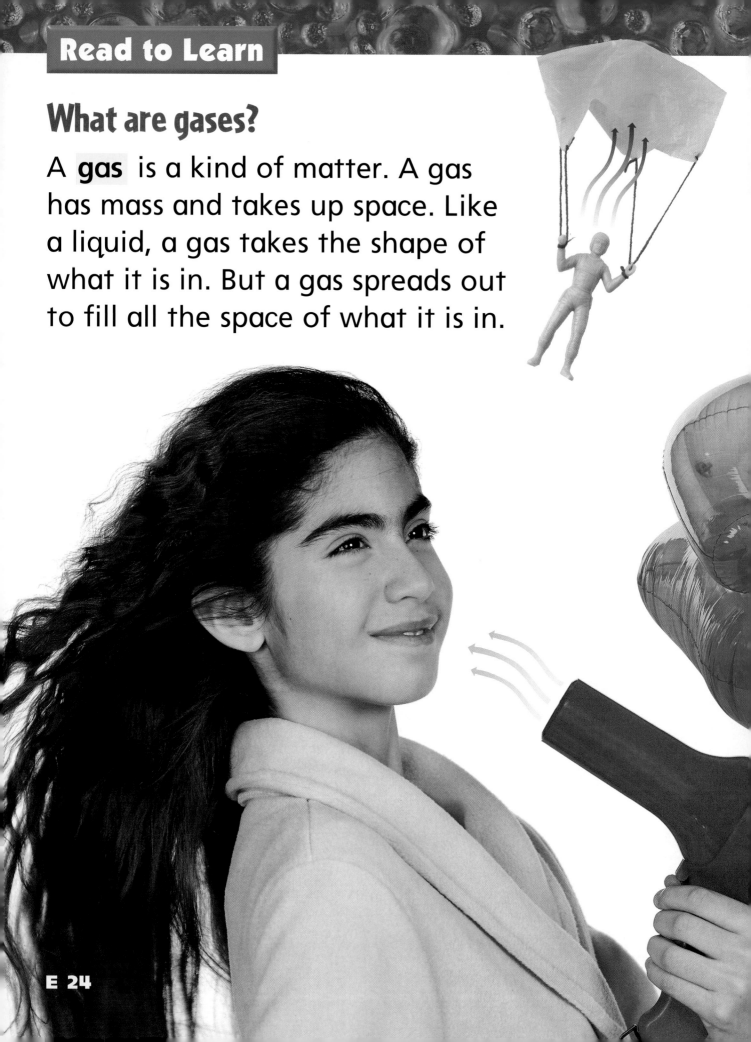

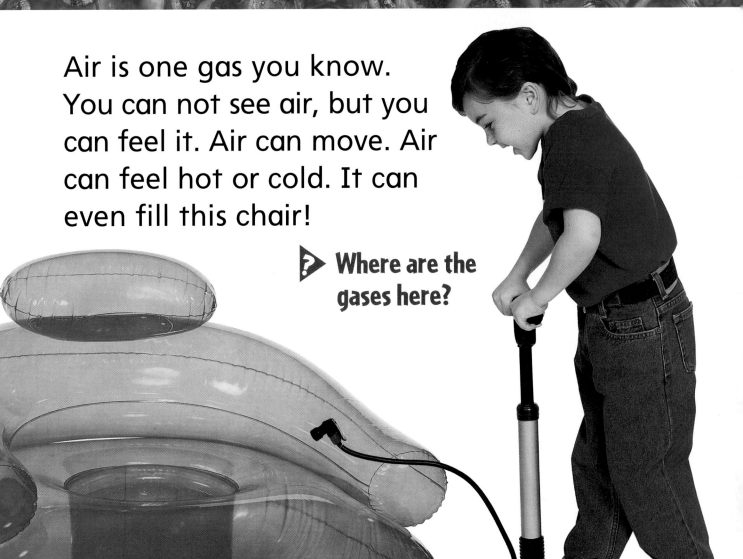

Air is one gas you know. You can not see air, but you can feel it. Air can move. Air can feel hot or cold. It can even fill this chair!

Where are the gases here?

Stop and Think

1. How are gases alike?
2. How do we know air is real?

MORE TO READ Read **Air Is All Around You** by Franklyn M. Branley.

Solid Shapes

Shape is a property of solids. Look around you. Every solid has a shape. The shape helps you tell what it is.

sphere   cone   cube

Try This!

Use clay to make the shapes above. Make other shapes, too. Use your shapes to make something.

Mystery Bag

Sometimes you can tell what a thing is without looking at it. Find out how. Read *What's in the Bag?* by Pat McGuinne.

Try This!

Get a bag. Play "What's in the Bag?" with a partner.

WHAT'S
IN THE BAG?

by Pat McGuinne
Illustrated by Selina Alko

Science Newsroom CD-ROM
Choose **Balancing Act** to learn more about mass

E 27

Vocabulary

- ruler
- gas
- matter
- liquid
- solid
- mass
- balance
- measuring cup
- properties

Use each word once for items 1–9. Tell what kind of matter each picture shows.

1

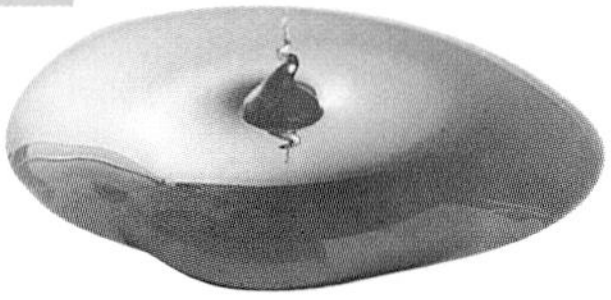

2

3

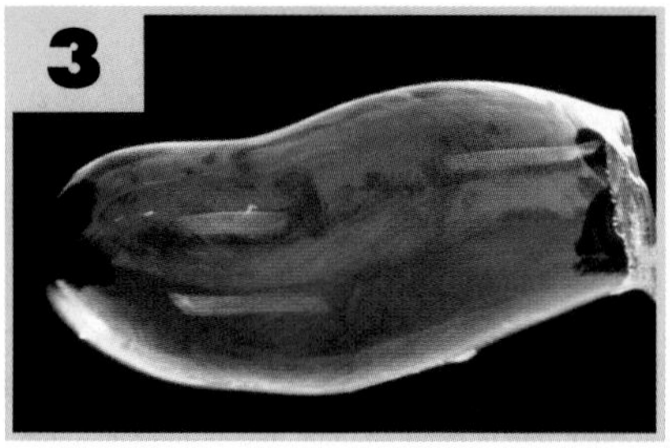

Tell what tool each picture shows.

4

5

6

Use this picture to complete each sentence.

7 The boy is made of ____.

8 The air in the tube has less ____ than water.

9 Cold and wet are ____ of water.

10 Tell what you know about the shape and space of liquids.

11 Tell what you know about the shape and space of gases.

Science Skill: Compare

12 How are these kinds of matter the same? How are they different?

Changes in
Matter

Vocabulary

mixture

float

sink

melt

freeze

Did You Ever Wonder?

What makes an icicle melt? Heat from the Sun can melt it. The icicle turns to water and drips to the ground. What else can melt?

Solids in Mixtures

Get Ready

This boy puts the parts together. What does he make?

Science Skill

You **draw a conclusion** when you use what you observe to explain what happens.

Explore Activity

What you need

paper

Can you put some solids together and take them apart?

scissors

What to do

1 Cut a paper into four pieces.

> **BE CAREFUL!** Scissors are sharp.

2 Find a friend whose pieces are a different color than yours. Mix the pieces together.

3 Try to pull your own pieces out of the mix. **Draw a conclusion** about paper that is mixed together.

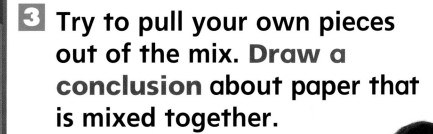

How can you change the shape and size of solids?

You can change the shape of some solids. You can bend them or fold them. But they are still made out of the same thing.

You can cut some solids, too. Then you have smaller pieces. But they are still made out of the same thing.

▷ **How did each solid change? How did each solid stay the same?**

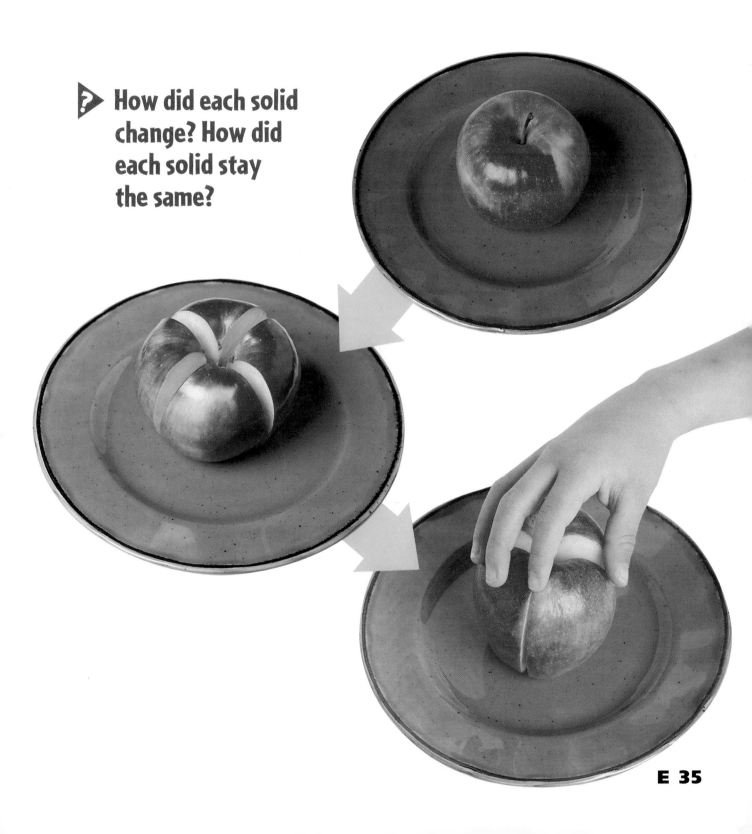

What is a mixture?

A **mixture** is two or more different things put together. Some mixtures are made of solids.

The things you put in a mixture do not change. You can mix beads in a jar. Then you can take each one out. They do not change.

▷ **What is each of these mixtures made of?**

Stop and Think

1. How can you change the shape and size of solids?

2. What is a mixture?

AT THE COMPUTER

Visit **www.mhscience02.com** to find out more about mixtures.

Solids and Liquids in Water

Get Ready

The leaf is on top of the water. The coins are at the bottom. What will happen to other solids in water?

Science Skill

You **predict** when you use what you know to tell what will happen.

Explore Activity

What happens when you put some solids in water?

penny

cork

salt

spoon

What to do

1 **Predict** what will happen to a penny, a cork, and some salt when you put them in water.

2 Place the penny and cork in the water one at a time. What happens?

3 Place some salt in the water. What happens?

4 Were your predictions correct? Talk about it.

pan of water

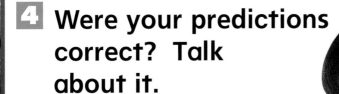

What happens to some solids in water?

You can put solids and liquids together. That makes a mixture. Some solids in water break up into smaller pieces. This drink mix breaks up in water. But it is still there. It makes a mixture.

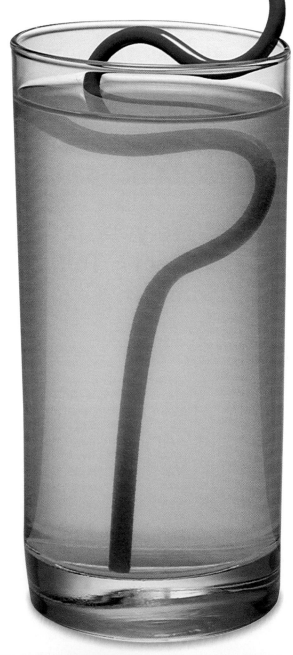

Many solids do not break up in water. Some solids **float**. They stay on top of the water. Other solids **sink**. They fall to the bottom of the water.

▷ **What happens to these solids in water?**

What happens to some liquids in water?

When you put any liquid in water, you make a mixture. Some liquids, such as vinegar, mix with water. The vinegar here spreads all through the water.

vinegar and water

oil and water

Other liquids do not mix with water. Oil is a liquid. It floats on top of water. But oil and water still make a mixture.

▶ Look at the blue liquid in water. Tell what happens to it.

Stop and Think

1. What happens to some solids in water?

2. What happens to some liquids in water?

MORE TO READ Read **Floating and Sinking** by Jack Challoner.

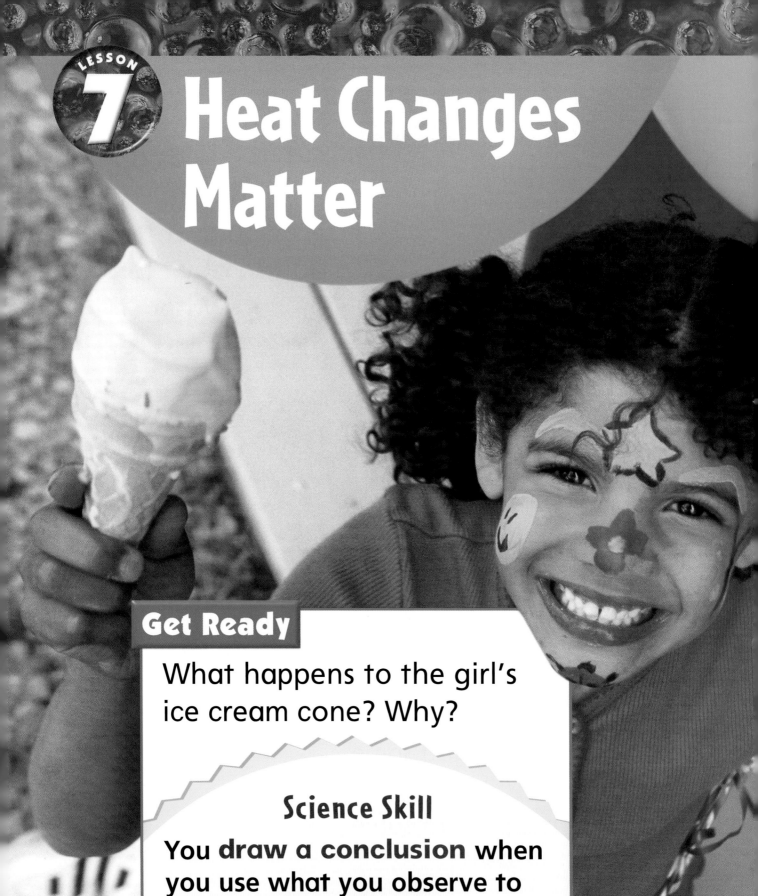

Heat Changes Matter

Get Ready

What happens to the girl's ice cream cone? Why?

Science Skill

You **draw a conclusion** when you use what you observe to explain what happens.

Explore Activity

What happens to ice in a warm place?

two paper plates

two ice cubes

What to do

1 Put ice on each paper plate.

2 Put one plate in a warm place. Put the other in a cool place. Predict what will happen to each.

3 Wait about 15 minutes. Compare the ice on each plate. **Draw a conclusion** about what happens to ice in a warm place.

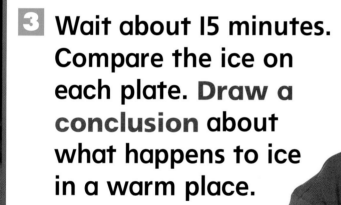

How does a solid change to a liquid?

When a solid gets enough heat, it will **melt**. Melt means to change from a solid to a liquid.

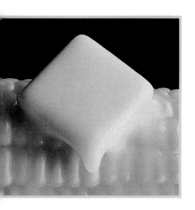

Some solids melt with a little heat. Other solids melt only with a lot of heat. Ice is a solid. When ice melts, it changes to liquid water.

▶ **How are solids changing to liquids in each picture?**

How does a liquid change to a solid?

Heat can leave a liquid. The liquid gets cool. When it loses enough heat, it changes to a solid.

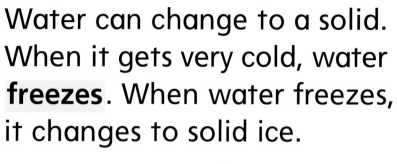

Water can change to a solid. When it gets very cold, water **freezes**. When water freezes, it changes to solid ice.

▶ **Tell how liquids change to solids in each picture.**

Stop and Think

1. When do solids change to liquids?

2. When do liquids change to solids?

HOME ACTIVITY

Find foods that you melt. Find foods that you freeze.

Mix Colors

Color is a property of matter. When you mix colors together, you get a new color.

Try This!

Get red, yellow, and blue paint. Get paper, too. What happens when you mix yellow paint with blue paint? Red with yellow? Red with blue?

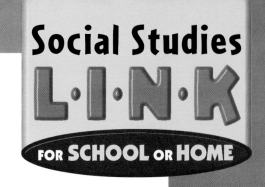
Origami Shapes

In Japan, people fold paper to make shapes. This art is called origami.

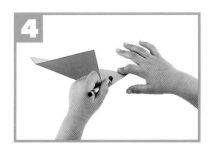

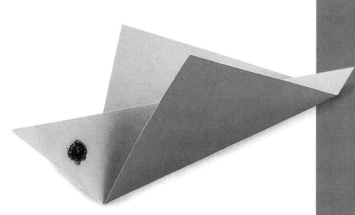

Try This!

Make a grasshopper.

1. Fold a square piece of paper to make a triangle.

2. Make a fold at an angle as shown.

3. Make the same fold on the other side.

4. Give your grasshopper eyes.

Vocabulary

float

melt

freeze

sink

mixture

Use each word once for items 1–5.

Science Ideas

6 What happens to some solids in water?

7 What happens to some liquids in water?

8 How does a solid stay the same when you cut it? How does it change?

Science Skill: Predict

9 Predict what will happen to the apple and grapes if you put them together.

10 Predict what will happen to the icicles in the sunshine.

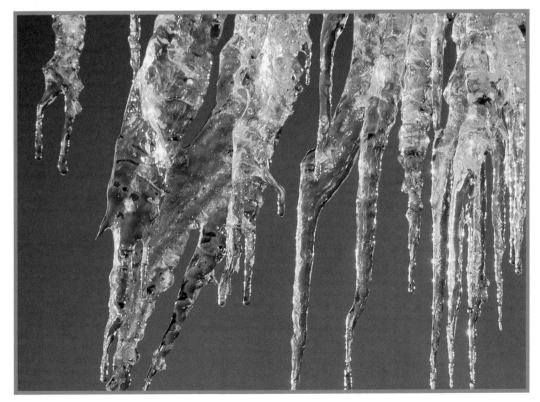

A Cool Idea!

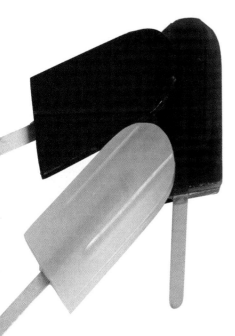

In 1905, young Frank Epperson made some soda pop. He mixed it with a stick. He left the pop in a glass outside. He left the stick in the glass, too. That night, it got very cold.

The next day, Frank pulled on the stick. The pop came out with it. The pop was frozen. Frank tasted the frozen pop. It tasted great. Frank had made the first ice pop. Later, Frank began a business making ice pops.

 What happened to the soda pop Frank left outside?

Frank's granddaughter feeds him an ice pop.

AT THE COMPUTER

Visit **www.mhscience02.com**
to find out more about inventors.

SCIENCE Workshop

1. Make a book about matter.

- Write what matter is.
- Write three properties of matter.
- Write about solids, liquids, and gases.

2. Draw a picture of each thing:

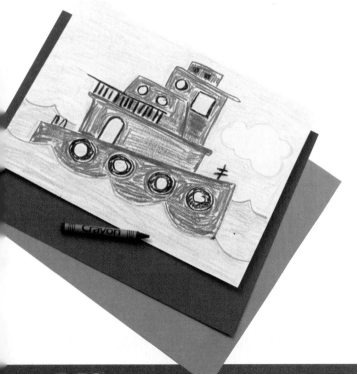

- a mixture of solids
- a mixture of oil and water
- something that floats
- something that sinks
- something that melts

UNIT
F

On the Move

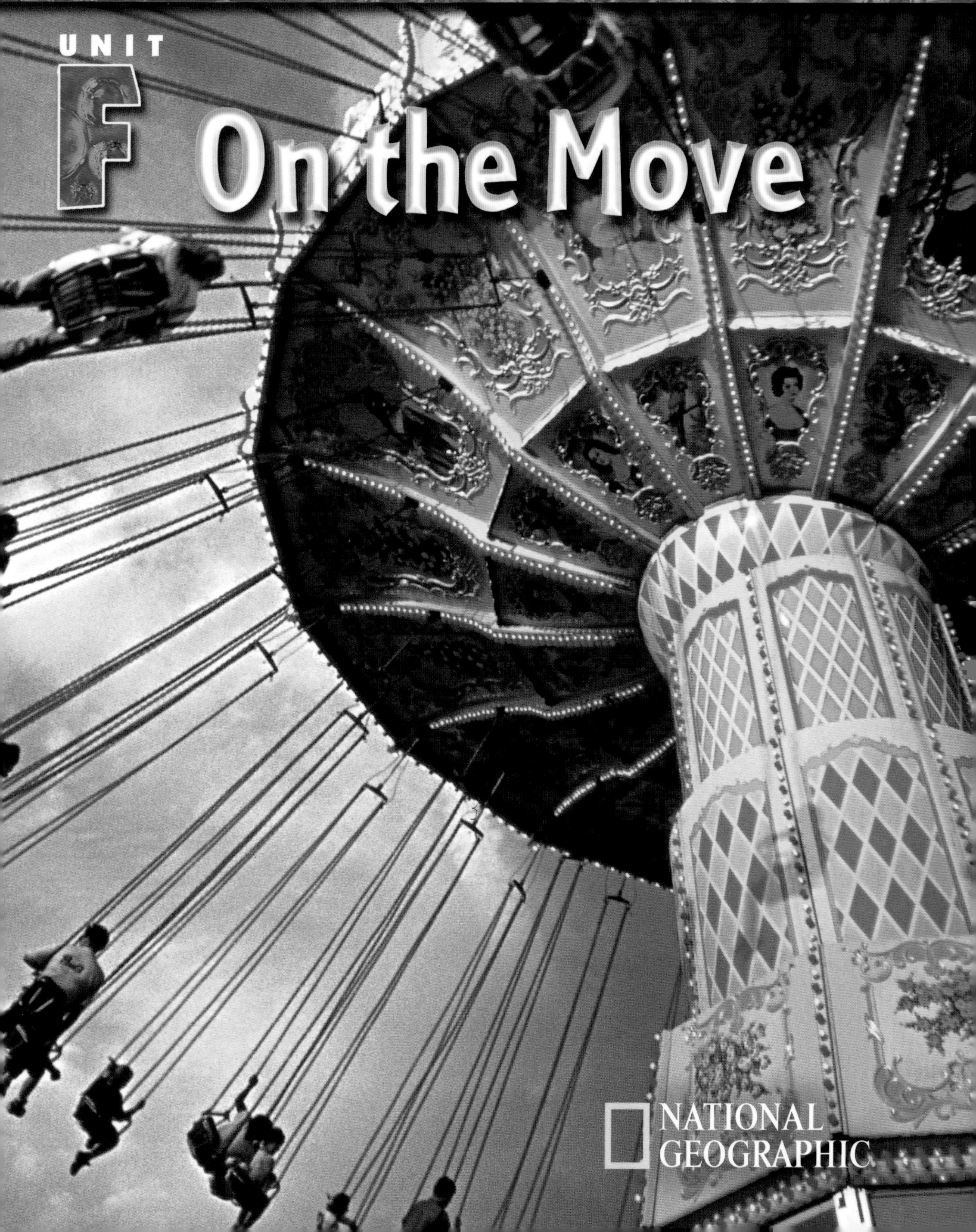

NATIONAL GEOGRAPHIC

On the Move

Force and Motion

Did You Ever Wonder?

How do skaters move? Ice skates have metal blades. They glide over the ice. What are some ways skaters move across ice?

1 Things Move

Get Ready

The boy has a scooter. What must the boy do to move it?

Science Skill

You **observe** when you use your senses to find out about things.

Explore Activity

How can you move things?

small things

What to do

1 Pick something to move.

2 Write or tell what you did to move it.

3 Do the same for the other things. What did you **observe** about how to move them?

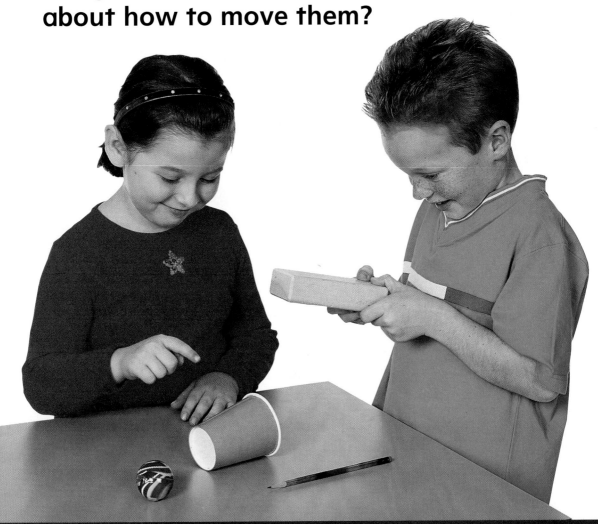

What makes things move?

You can move something with a **push**. A push moves something away from you.

push

pull

You can also move something with a **pull**. A pull moves something closer to you.

F 6

A push or a pull is a **force**. It takes a force to move something. It takes a little force to move something light. It takes a lot of force to move something heavy.

▷ **Which children pull?**
Which children push?

pull and push

How can you tell about where something is?

Position is the place where something is. Position words tell where a thing is. Inside and outside are position words. Top and bottom are, too.

top

bottom

inside

outside

Here is Aunt Edna. When she knits, her cats play.

▶ **What words tell where the cats are?**

Stop and Think

1. How can you move things?

2. What are position words? Name some of them.

AT THE COMPUTER

Visit **www.mhscience02.com** to find out more about forces.

2 Measure Movement

Get Ready

The woman jumps. How can you find out how far she jumps?

Science Skill

You **measure** when you find out how far something moves.

Explore Activity

How can you measure how far something moves?

What you need

ruler

pencil

paper

eraser

What to do

1 Put the eraser on top of the paper. Mark its place with an X.

2 Have a partner move the eraser on the paper.

3 **Measure** how far the eraser was moved. What did you do to measure?

How can you measure how far things move?

You can use a ruler to measure how far things move.

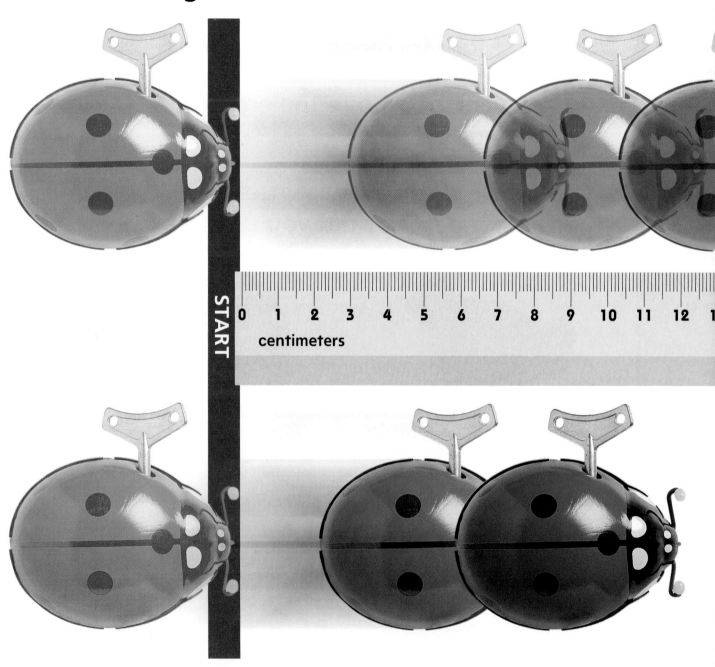

START

0 1 2 3 4 5 6 7 8 9 10 11 12 1

centimeters

You put the end of the ruler with 0 at the start. Then you line up the ruler to where the thing moved. The numbers show how far it moved.

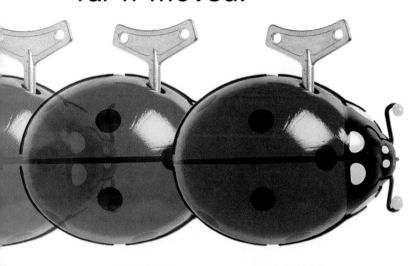

▷ **How far did the toys go?**

14　15　16　17　18　19　20　21　22　23　24　25　26　27　28　29　30　31　32　33

Stop and Think

1. How can you find out how far something moves?

2. What can you use to find out how far something moves?

The Ways Things Move

Get Ready

The people go up and down. How can you find out other ways things move?

Science Skill

You **investigate** when you make a plan and try it out.

Explore Activity

What you need

cup

spring toy

ball

Do all things move the same way?

What to do

1. Look at each thing. Will each one move the same way?

2. **Investigate** how each thing moves. Push or pull each one.

3. Did each thing move the same way? Talk about it.

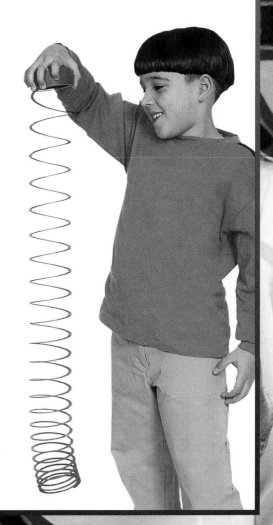

What ways do things move?

Things can move in many ways. Some things move up and down. Some move back and forth. Some move straight. And some move round and round.

▷ **Tell how these children move.**

What can change the ways things move?

A force can change the way a thing moves.

Throw a ball. It starts to move.

Catch a ball. It
stops moving.

Kick a moving ball.
The force makes the ball
change direction.

▶ **Does a push or pull change
the way each thing moves?**

Stop and Think

1. What are some ways things move?

2. What changes the way a thing moves?

 **MORE
TO READ**   Read **Who Hops?** by Katie Davis.

Go Find It

People use position words to help each other find things. They use these words at home, at school, at work, and at play.

Try This!

Hide a book in a room. Tell someone how to find the book. Here are some position words you can use.

right	left
under	above
inside	outside
in front of	behind
next to	

Science Newsroom CD-ROM
Choose **Gravity** to learn more about a special force.

Which Moves Far?

When you throw something, it moves. Some things move farther than other things. How can you compare how far things move?

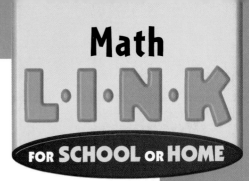

Try This!

Make paper planes of many shapes and sizes. Throw each one. Measure how far each one moves. Write each measure in a chart.

START

Vocabulary

push

pull

force

position

Use each word once for items 1–4.

1

2

3 When an object moves, it changes ____.

4 To move something heavy, you need a lot of ____.

Science Ideas

5 Tell about the position of the cat.

6 How could you find out how far the woman jumps?

7 What makes the ball start to move?

Science Skill: Classify

Tell how each thing moves.

8

9

10

READ
My Kite by Cynthia Rothman

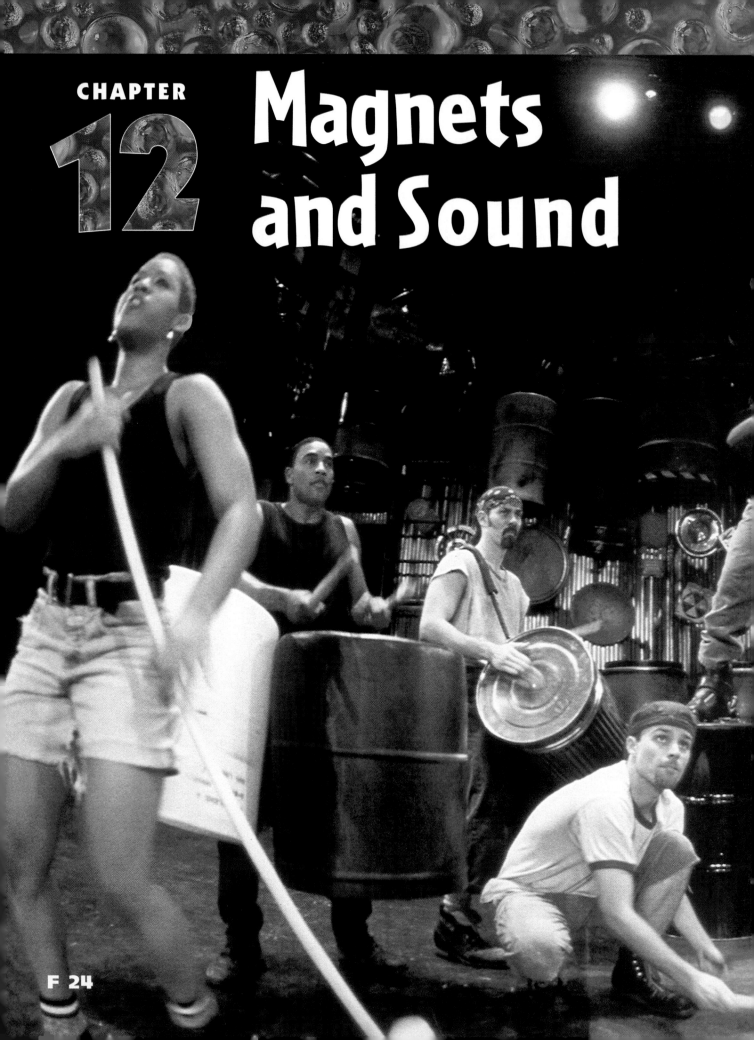

12

Magnets and Sound

Vocabulary

attract

poles

repel

vibrate

Did You Ever Wonder?

Did you ever wonder how sound is made? Moving things make sound. What do these people move to make sound? How else can you make sound?

F 25

Things Magnets Move

Get Ready

What keeps the toy car from falling?

Science Skill

You **draw a conclusion** when you use what you know to explain something.

Explore Activity

magnet

What will move to a magnet?

What to do

1 Draw each item in a chart.

2 Hold a magnet near each thing. Does each thing move to the magnet? Check yes or no in the chart.

classroom items

3 Draw a **conclusion** about which things move to a magnet.

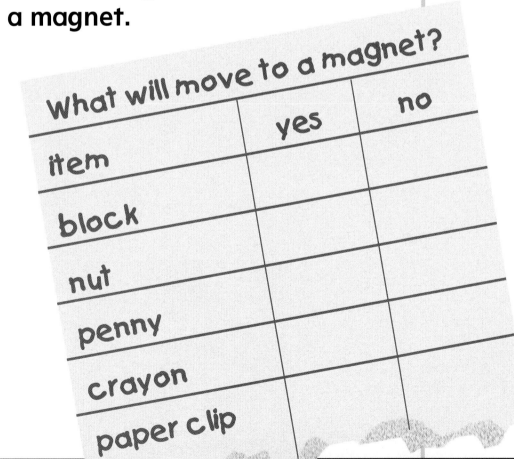

What will move to a magnet?

item	yes	no
block		
nut		
penny		
crayon		
paper clip		

What does a magnet do?

A magnet can pull, or **attract**, some things to it. These things have iron in them. Iron is a metal that magnets attract.

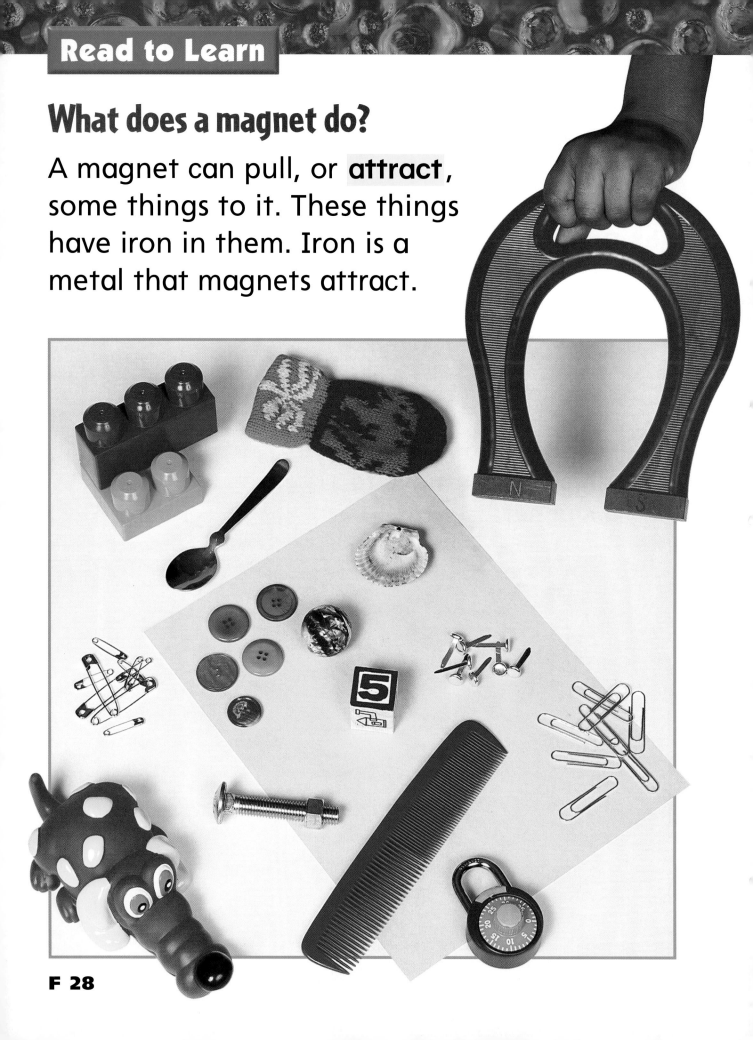

The things on this horseshoe magnet all have iron in them. The force of the magnet attracts them.

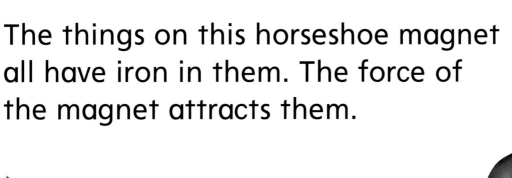 **Which things move to the magnet? Why?**

How are magnets alike and different?

All magnets attract things with iron in them. They do not attract things made of wood or glass. They do not attract things made of plastic.

bar magnets

refrigerator magnet

Clean your room!

wand magnet

Magnets can be many sizes, shapes, and colors. Some magnets are strong. Others are weak. A strong magnet has a greater pulling force than a weak magnet.

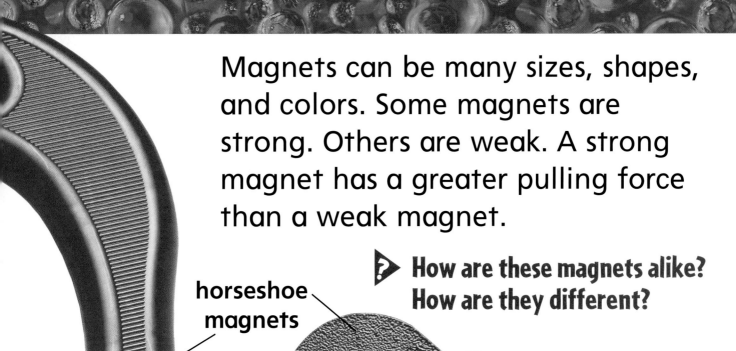

horseshoe magnets

How are these magnets alike? How are they different?

ring magnet

Stop and Think

1. What will move to a magnet?
2. Are all magnets the same? Talk about it.

AT THE COMPUTER

Visit **www.mhscience02.com** to find out more about magnets.

A Magnet's Poles

Get Ready

The girl wants to find out if all parts of a magnet pull the same. What do you think her plan is?

Science Skill

You **investigate** when you make a plan and try it out.

Explore Activity

Where on a magnet is the pull strongest?

bar magnet

paper clips

What to do

1 **Investigate** where a magnet's pull is strongest. Make a plan.

2 Try out your plan.

3 Draw the magnet. Circle the parts where the magnet's pull is strongest. Tell how you know.

What are the parts of a magnet?

A magnet has two **poles**. Poles are where a magnet's pull is strongest. One pole is called the north pole. It is marked N. The other is called the south pole. It is marked S.

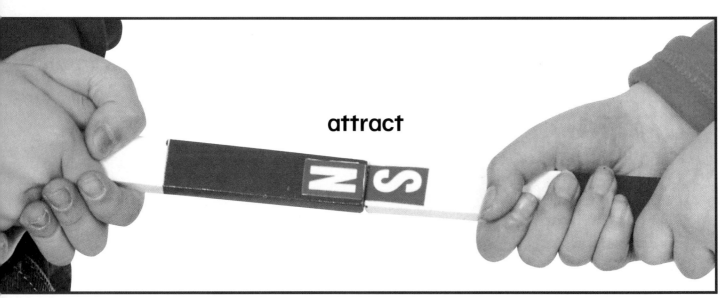

attract

If you put an N pole next to an S pole, the magnets attract.

If you put an N pole next to an N pole, the magnets **repel**. Repel means to push away. Alike poles repel.

▷ **What would happen if you put two S poles together?**

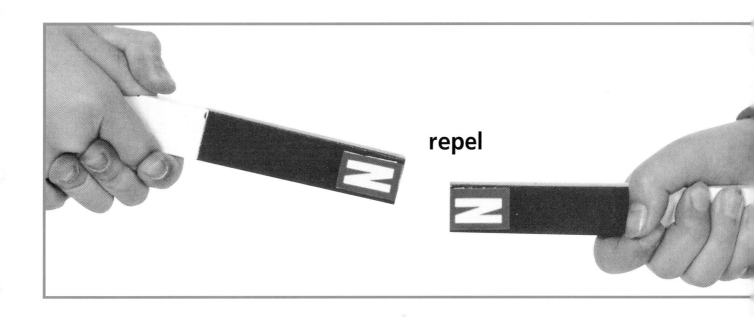

repel

Stop and Think

1. What do N and S mean on a magnet?
2. What can happen when the poles of two magnets are put together?

AT THE COMPUTER

Visit **www.mhscience02.com** to find out more about magnets.

Things Magnets Pull Through

Get Ready

This game uses a magnet. How does it work?

Science Skill

You **observe** when you find out how things work.

Explore Activity

Can a magnet pull through things?

book

magnet

paper clip

What to do

1 Hold a magnet under a page in a book. Put a clip on top of the page. Move the magnet.

2 Try the same thing with the cover. Try the whole book.

3 Can a magnet pull through things? Tell what you **observe**.

What can magnets pull through?

A magnet can pull through many things. It can pull through paper and glass. It can even pull through air. The pulling force is strong close to a magnet. It is weaker away from a magnet.

A magnet can pull through cardboard.

A magnet can pull through glass.

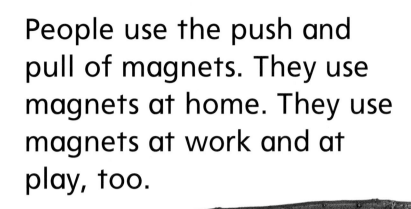

People use the push and pull of magnets. They use magnets at home. They use magnets at work and at play, too.

▷ **How is this girl using a magnet?**

A magnet can pull through water.

Stop and Think

1. What are some things magnets can pull through?

2. How do people use magnets?

HOME ACTIVITY Look around your home for magnets.

Moving Things Make Sound

Get Ready

This boy plays a guitar. How do you think the sounds are made?

guitar

Science Skill

You **infer** when you use what you know to figure out how something works.

Explore Activity

Can you make sound by using a rubber band?

What you need

plastic bowl

rubber band

goggles

What to do

1 Put the rubber band around the bowl.

> **BE CAREFUL!** Wear goggles.

2 Pull the rubber band. Let go. What do you see? What do you hear?

3 Pull it again. Stop the rubber band from moving. What happens? What do you **infer** made the sound?

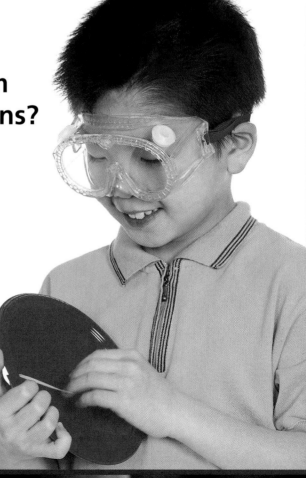

How is sound made?

Sound is what you hear. If you pull on a harp's string, it **vibrates**. Vibrate means to move back and forth quickly.

harp

When a string vibrates, it makes sound. The things here make sound when you pull, bang, hit, or blow into them.

horn

drum

Anything that makes sound vibrates. When a thing stops vibrating, the sound stops, too.

triangle

> **How are sounds made here?**

Stop and Think

1. What does vibrate mean?
2. When does something stop making sound?

HOME ACTIVITY List some sounds you hear in your neighborhood.

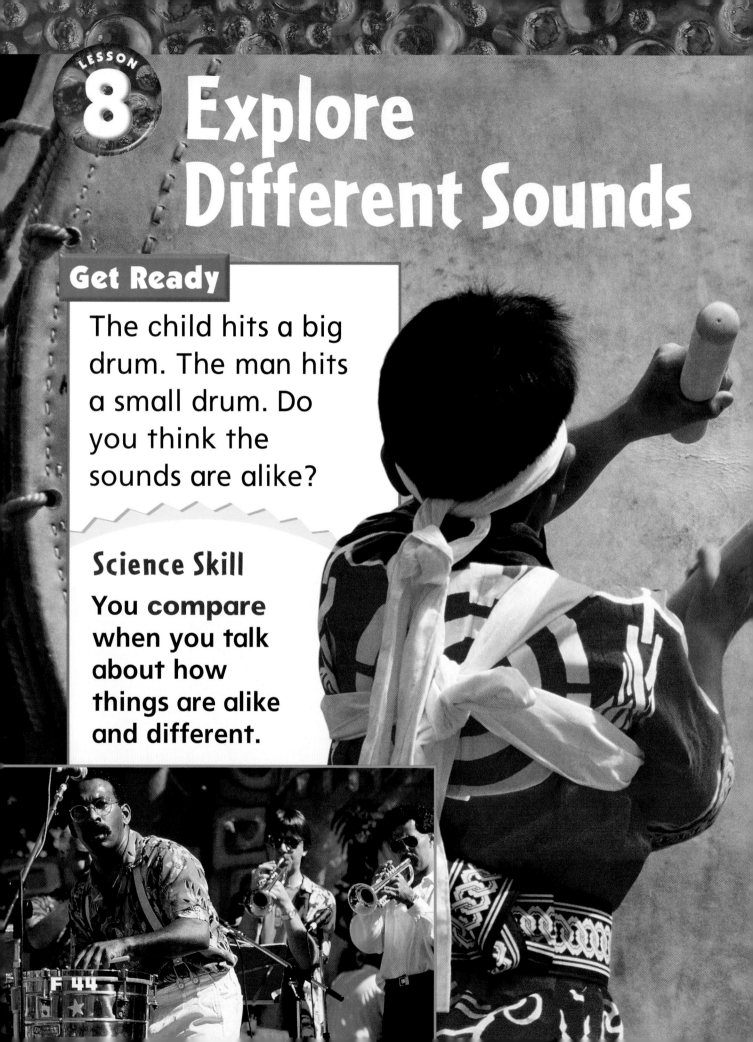

Explore Different Sounds

Get Ready

The child hits a big drum. The man hits a small drum. Do you think the sounds are alike?

Science Skill

You **compare** when you talk about how things are alike and different.

Explore Activity

Can you find sounds that are the same?

What to do

1 Shake each sound maker. **Compare** the sounds you hear.

2 Which ones sound the same? Make pairs.

3 Which do not sound the same? Tell about the sound made by each sound maker.

How are sounds different?

There are many kinds of sounds. Some are soft. Some are loud.

A whisper is a soft sound. A fire truck makes a loud sound.

fire truck

whistle

whisper

Some sounds are high.
Some sounds are low.

A whistle makes a high
sound. A bullfrog
makes a low sound.

▶ **Tell about these sounds.**

bullfrog

Ribbit!

What can you find out from sounds?

You know things by their sounds. A cat's meow is not like a dog's bark. A phone's ring is not like a doorbell's ring.

Sounds can tell you things. A laugh tells you someone is happy. A fire truck's sound tells you to let the truck pass.

▷ **Look at the pictures on these pages. What does each sound tell you?**

Stop and Think

1. Are all sounds the same? Talk about it.

2. What does the sound of a fire alarm tell you?

 **MORE TO READ** Read **Jungle Drum** by Deanna Wundrow.

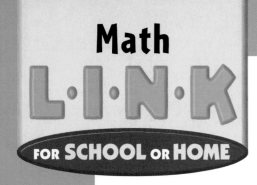

Pick It Up

You can compare how strong different magnets are. You can count how many paper clips each magnet picks up.

Try This!

Try to pick up paper clips with two different magnets. Count how many clips each magnet picks up. Which magnet is stronger?

The Sound of a Bell

Bell sounds can mean different things. Find out about the sound of one bell. Read *The Third Bell* by Catherine McCafferty.

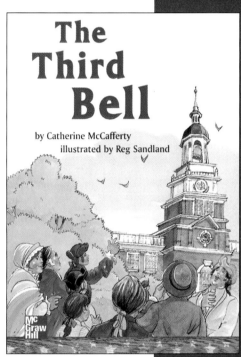

The Third Bell

by Catherine McCafferty
illustrated by Reg Sandland

Try This!

Draw bells you have seen or know about. Tell what each bell sound means.

Vocabulary

attract

poles

repel

vibrate

Use each word once for items 1–4.

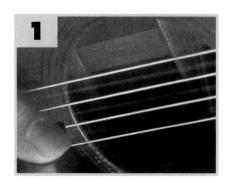

1

2

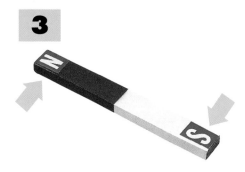

3

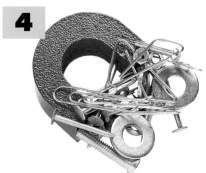

4

Science Ideas

5 Which things have iron in them? Tell how you know.

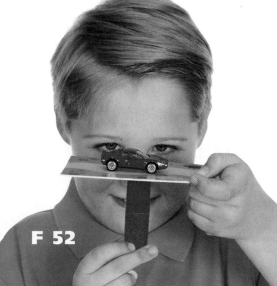

6 How does the car move?

7 What happens when the strings vibrate?

8 Tell how these sounds are different.

Science Skill: Communicate

9 Use the graph. Where does the magnet pull more clips? How can you tell?

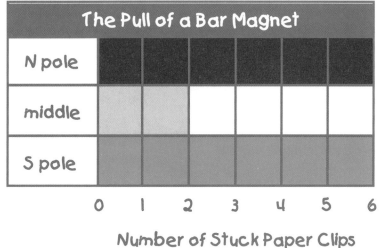

The Pull of a Bar Magnet						
N pole						
middle						
S pole						

0 1 2 3 4 5 6

Number of Stuck Paper Clips

Richie Stachowski

Inventor

Have you ever had an idea for a new tool? Richie Stachowski did. He made a new tool. It helps people talk under water. He made it when he was only ten years old.

Richie Stachowski with his first invention, the Water Talkie™

Richie's tool is called the Water Talkie™. He made it because it is hard to speak clearly in water. Richie tried different ways to make sound in water. Then he made the Water Talkie™. Today, people use Water Talkies™ to talk under water.

What does Richie's tool do?

Richie and his parents work on a new invention, special underwater glasses. Their dog, Abigail, tries them on.

The final product!

 **AT THE COMPUTER** Visit **www.mhscience02.com** for more amazing stories and facts.

SCIENCE
Workshop

1. **Tell about a game** you play with a ball. Answer these questions about the ball.

- Do you push or pull it?

- Where does it go? Use position words to tell.

- How does it move?

- What would you use to measure how far it moves?

- What can change the way it moves?

2. **Make an instrument.** How does it work? What sounds does it make?

For Your Reference

Skills Handbook

Science Handbook

Health Handbook

Glossary

Science Skill Builder 1

Observe

You **observe** with your senses. You see, hear, touch, smell, and taste.

What you need

classroom
objects

What to do

1. Pick an object in your classroom.

2. Look at it. Touch it. Smell it. Does it make sound?

3. What did you **observe** about the object? Talk about it.

4. Observe other objects.

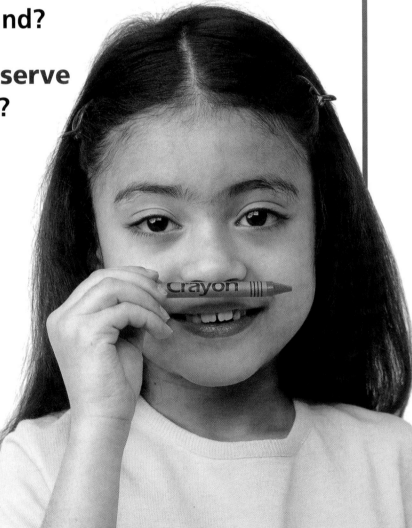

Science Skill Builder 2

Compare

You **compare** when you observe how things are alike and different.

What to do

1. **Compare** the orange and apple.

2. Name two ways they are alike.

3. Name two ways they are different.

4. Compare other things in your classroom.

Measure

You **measure** to find out the size or amount of something.

What you need

same-size paper clips

same-size pencils

What to do

1 Place paper clips across your desk like this. How many paper clips wide is your desk?

2 Use pencils to **measure** your desk. How many pencils wide is your desk?

3 What else could you use to measure the desk? Try it.

Classify

You **classify** when you make groups that are alike.

What to do

1 Look at these buttons.

2 **Classify** the buttons by color. Draw the groups.

3 Find a new way to classify the buttons. Draw the groups.

Communicate

You **communicate** to share ideas. You can talk, write, or draw to communicate.

What to do

1 How many boys and girls are in class today? Count them.

2 **Communicate** this information. Make a graph like the girl did.

3 Talk about your graph.

crayons

drawing paper

Put Things in Order

You put things in **order** when you tell what happens first, next, and last.

What to do

1 Think of a favorite story.

2 Draw three pictures to show what happens first, next, and last.

3 Mix up your pictures. Have a friend put them in **order**.

crayons

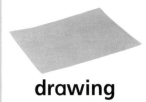

drawing paper

Infer

You **infer** when you use what you know to figure something out.

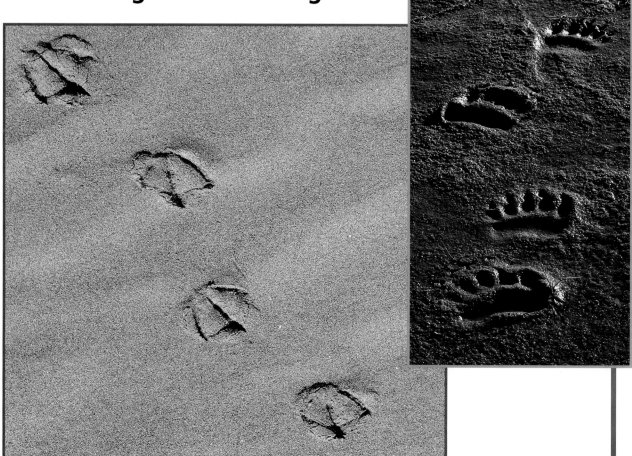

What to do

1 What do you know about these footprints?

2 Use what you know to **infer** which set of footprints the bird made. Talk about it.

Make a Model

You **make a model** to show how a place looks or how a thing works. This model shows what the girl's schoolyard looks like.

What to do

1 Think of a place in your school. Plan a model of that place.

2 Decide how to make the model look real.

3 **Make a model.** Share it with others.

Predict

You **predict** when you use what you observe to tell what will happen next.

What to do

1 Look at the picture. What do you observe?

2 Draw a picture to show what you **predict** will happen next.

Investigate

You **investigate** when you make a plan and then try it out.

What to do

1 **Investigate** the easiest way to get from your classroom to the cafeteria.

2 Make a plan to find out which way is easiest. Share your plan with others.

3 Try out your plan.

Draw a Conclusion

You **draw a conclusion** when you use what you observe to explain what happens.

What to do

1 Look at the picture. What do you observe?

2 Can you **draw a conclusion** about what's wrong here? Talk about it.

Save and Recycle

We should not waste things.

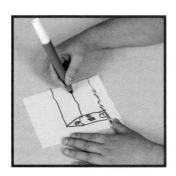

Use no more than you need.

Don't leave the water on.

Recycle as much as you can.

Use things more than once.

Care of Animals

Here are ways to care for animals.

- Give pets food and water. Give them a safe place to live, too.

- Be kind to pets. Handle them with care.

- Don't touch wild animals. They may bite, sting, or scratch you.

- Do not touch things in places where wild animals live.

Care of Plants

Here are ways to care for plants.

- Give plants water and sunlight.

- Ask the teacher before you touch or eat a plant. Some plants can make you very sick!

- Do not dig up plants or pick flowers. Let plants grow where they are.

Clean Up

We need to keep work places clean.

Let an adult clean up broken glass.

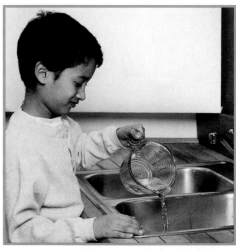

Pour water into a sink, not into a trash can.

Put food in plastic bags. This keeps bugs away.

Don't get paint or food on you.

How to Measure

You can use many things to measure.

This string is about 8 paper clips long.

This string is about 3 pencils long.

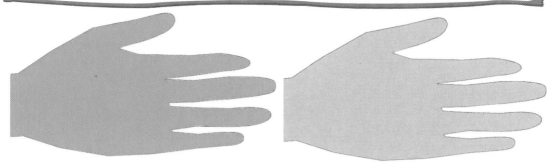

This string is about 2 hands long.

Try This!

● Measure some string. Tell how you did it.

● Can you measure string with these paper clips? Why or why not?

Units of Measurement

There are other ways to measure. You can use centimeters (cm) or meters (m). These are called units of measurement.

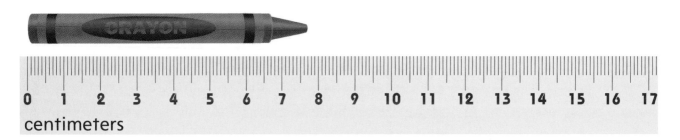

The crayon is about 8 centimeters long. We write this as 8 cm.

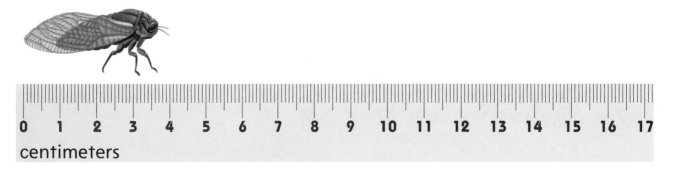

The insect is about 4 centimeters long. We write this as 4 cm.

Try This!

- How long is this pencil?

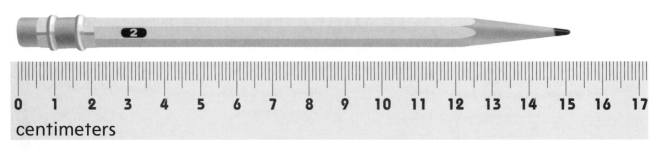

Use a Ruler

You can use a ruler to measure this leaf. Line up the end of the leaf with the 0 on the ruler. The leaf is about 11 centimeters, or 11 cm.

Try This!

Estimate how long each object is. Use a ruler to measure.

Object	Estimate	Measure
scissors	about ___ cm	about ___ cm
penny	about ___ cm	about ___ cm
toy car	about ___ cm	about ___ cm

Use a Thermometer

A thermometer measures temperature.

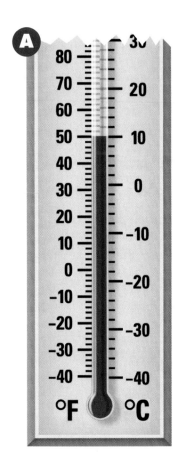
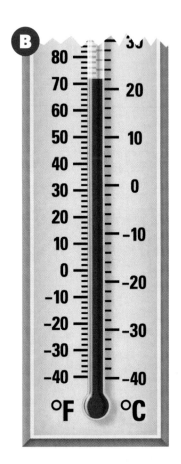

It gets warmer. The liquid in a thermometer moves up.

It gets cooler. The liquid in a thermometer moves down.

Which thermometer shows a warmer temperature? How can you tell?

A thermometer has marks with numbers.

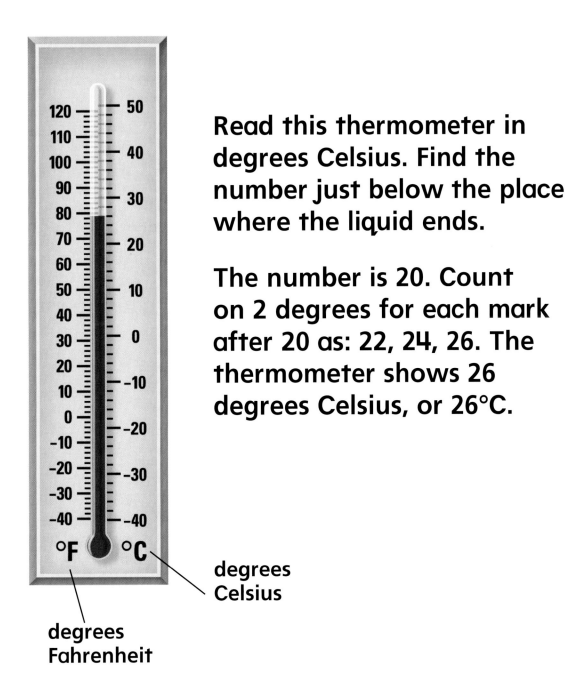

degrees
Celsius

degrees
Fahrenheit

Read this thermometer in degrees Celsius. Find the number just below the place where the liquid ends.

The number is 20. Count on 2 degrees for each mark after 20 as: 22, 24, 26. The thermometer shows 26 degrees Celsius, or 26°C.

Try This!

What temperatures are shown on page R20?

Use a Measuring Cup

Volume is the amount of space something takes up. You can use a measuring cup to find volume.

The marks on this cup show the number of milliliters. There are 500 milliliters (500 mL) of water in this cup.

measuring cup

Try This!

- Get 3 different small containers.

- Which holds the most? Which holds the least?

- Fill each container with water. Pour the water into the measuring cup. Find the volumes.

Use a Balance

A balance compares mass.

Place one object on each side of the balance. The object that has more mass will make that side of the balance go down. The object that has less mass will make that side of the balance go up.

- Place 2 objects on a balance. Which has more mass?

- Put 3 objects in order from least mass to most mass. Use the balance to check.

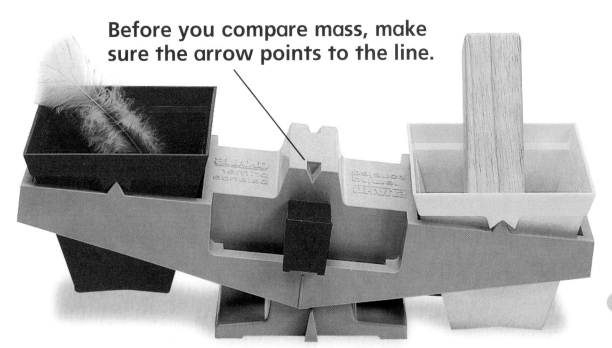

Before you compare mass, make sure the arrow points to the line.

Use a Clock

A clock measures time.

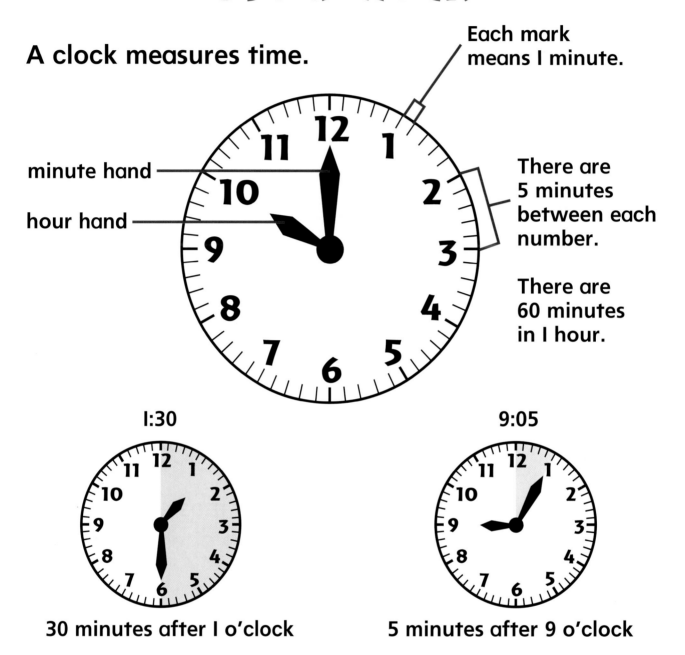

Each mark means 1 minute.

minute hand

hour hand

There are 5 minutes between each number.

There are 60 minutes in 1 hour.

1:30

30 minutes after 1 o'clock

9:05

5 minutes after 9 o'clock

Try This!

How long do you think it takes to write your name 5 times? Have a friend time you.

Use a Hand Lens

A hand lens makes objects seem larger.

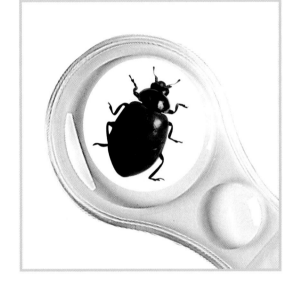

First, move the lens away from the object. Stop when the object looks fuzzy.

Next, move the lens a little closer to the object. Stop when the object looks clear.

Try This!

- Observe each bug here. Use a hand lens.

- How many legs do you see on the bugs?

- What else can you see?

Use a Computer

A computer is a tool that can get information.

You can use CD-ROMs. They have a lot of information. You can fit many books on one CD-ROM!

You can also use the Internet. The Internet links your computer to ones far away.

Try This!

- Use the Internet. Visit www.mhscience02.com and learn more about science in your world.

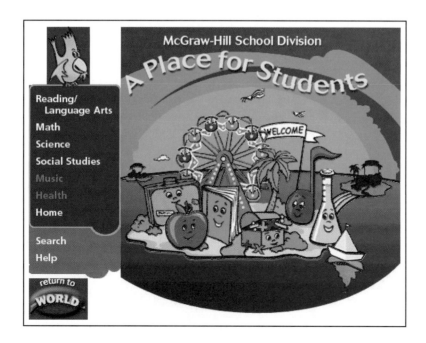

Your Body Parts

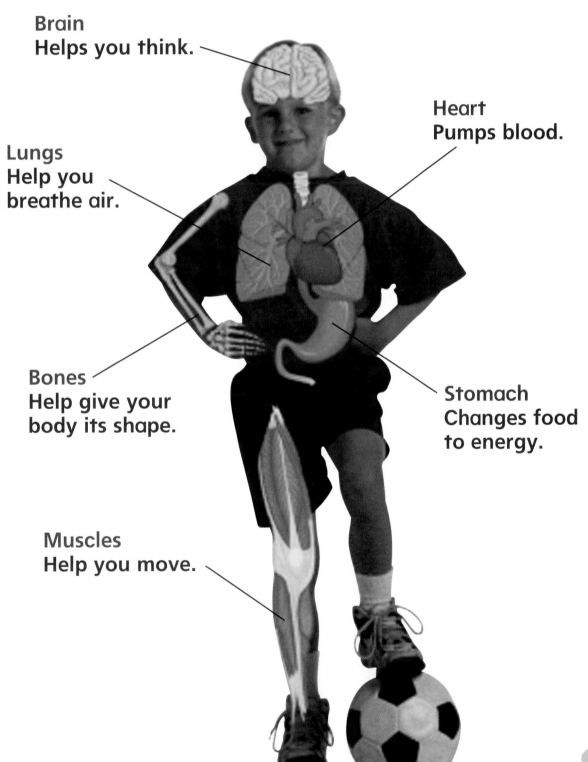

Brain
Helps you think.

Heart
Pumps blood.

Lungs
Help you
breathe air.

Bones
Help give your
body its shape.

Stomach
Changes food
to energy.

Muscles
Help you move.

Look Your Best

Keep your body clean.

Brush your teeth.

Sit and stand up tall.

Be Active and Rest

Be active every day.

Be sure to get enough sleep and rest, too.

These things help you grow!

Eat Healthful Foods

Choose healthful foods.

Milk and fruit are
healthful foods.

So are bread and vegetables.

Healthful foods help
you grow, too.

Getting Along

Work and play well with others.

Respect one another's feelings.

Show others that you care.

Be Safe Indoors

Some things are dangerous.

DO NOT TOUCH!

DANGER!

Be Safe Outdoors

Stay Healthy

Some people can help you stay healthy as you grow.

Get a checkup every year!

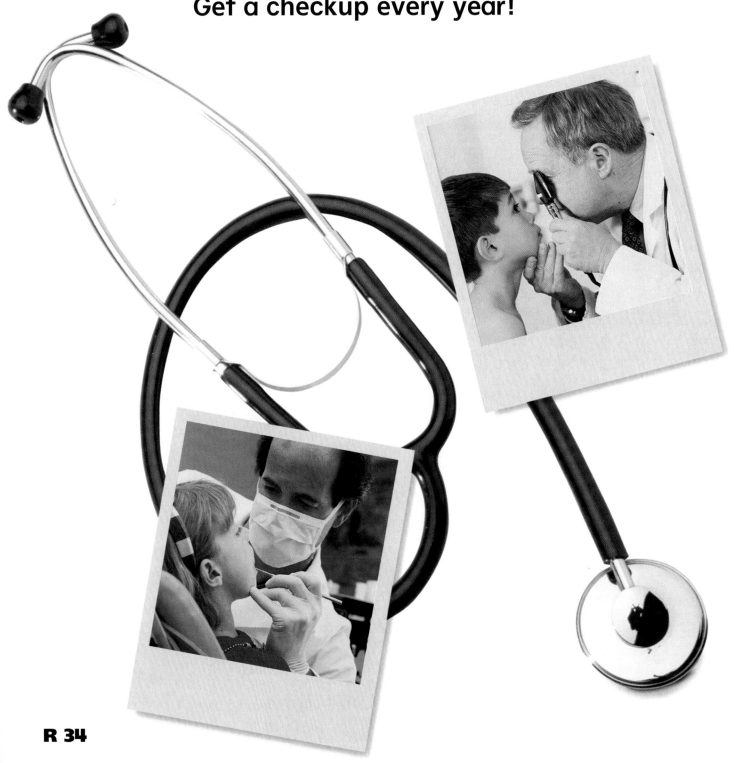

Glossary

A

amphibians animals that live in water and on land *(page B18)* **A frog is an amphibian.**

attract A magnet can attract some things to it. *(page F28)* **Iron is a metal that magnets attract.**

B

balance a tool that measures mass *(page E15)* **The side of the balance with more mass will go down.**

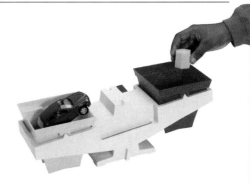

C

classify group things by how they are alike *(page B14)* **You can classify these animals.**

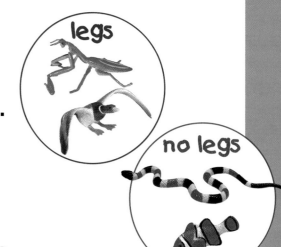
legs
no legs

AT THE COMPUTER Visit **www.mhscience02.com** to find out more about these words.

R 35

clouds made from lots of tiny drops of water that are in the air *(page C30)* **Rain or snow falls from clouds.**

communicate write, draw, or tell your ideas *(page A30)* **The boy draws to communicate what he observes.**

compare observe how things are alike or different *(page A10)* **The child compares the sponge and the ball.**

constellation a group of stars that makes a picture *(page C15)* **This constellation looks like a spoon.**

D

desert a place that gets very little rain *(page B40)* **A desert is very dry.**

draw a conclusion use what you observe to explain what happens *(page E16)* **You can draw a conclusion about what happened to this milk.**

F

fall the season after summer
(page C46) **In some places, leaves change color in the fall.**

float to stay on top of water
(page E41) **Some solids float.**

flowers the plant part that makes seeds *(page A48)*
Flowers make seeds.

food chain shows what animals eat *(page B35)* **The mouse is part of a food chain.**

force a push or a pull *(page F7)*
It takes a force to move something.

forest a place with many trees and other plants *(page B41)*
The trees in this forest are very tall.

freeze to change from a liquid to a solid *(page E49)* **When it gets very cold, water will freeze.**

fruit the plant part that grows around the seeds *(page A48)* **There are seeds inside this fruit.**

G

gas matter that spreads out to fill all the space of what it is in *(page E24)* **Bubbles have gas inside them.**

gills body parts used to breathe *(page B17)* **All fish have gills.**

gills

grassland a place with many grasses *(page B41)* **Many animals find food in a grassland.**

H

hatch to break out of an egg *(page B23)* **Ducks hatch out of eggs.**

I

infer use what you know to figure something out *(page A34)* **When a baby cries, you can infer that it needs something.**

insects animals with three body parts and six legs *(page B19)* **This animal is an insect.**

investigate make a plan and try it out *(page D44)* **The boy investigates what happens to water in stems.**

L

leaves plant part that makes food *(page A38)* **Leaves make food for a plant.**

liquid matter that flows and takes the shape of what you pour it in *(page E18)* **Water is a liquid.**

living thing something that grows, changes, and makes other living things like itself *(page A 12)* **A plant is a living thing.**

lungs body parts used to breathe *(page B16)* **All birds breathe with lungs.**

M

make a model make something to show how something looks *(page B38)* **You can make a model to show where a polar bear lives.**

mammals a group of animals with hair or fur that feed milk to their young *(page B12)* **This animal is a mammal.**

mass how much matter is in an object *(page E9)* **The metal ball has more mass.**

matter what makes up all things *(page E6)* **The block is made of matter.**

measure find out how far something moves, or how long, how much, or how warm something is *(page F10)* **You can measure how long the toy car is.**

---

measuring cup measures how much space a liquid takes up *(page E20)* **This is a measuring cup.**

---

melt to change from a solid to a liquid *(page E46)* **Heat makes the butter melt.**

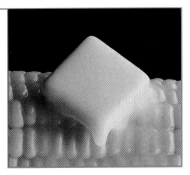

---

minerals the building blocks of rocks *(page D6)* **Minerals are a natural resource.**

---

mixture two or more different things put together *(page E36)* **This mixture is made of solids.**

natural resource something from Earth that people use *(page D8)* **Rock is a natural resource.**

nonliving things things that do not grow, eat, drink, or make more things like themselves *(page A13)* **Cars are nonliving things.**

O

observe see, hear, taste, touch, or smell *(page A4)* **You observe when you touch.**

ocean a very large body of salt water *(page B42)* **The ocean stretches out as far as you can see.**

order tell or show what happens first, next, or last *(page B32)* **The pictures are in order.**

oxygen a part of air that people need to live *(page D25)* **We breathe in oxygen from air.**

P

planet Earth is a planet that moves around the Sun. *(page C18)* **Earth is sometimes called the blue planet.**

poles where a magnet's pull is strongest *(page F34)* **A magnet has two poles.**

pollution harmful things in the air, water, or land *(page D40)* **Pollution happens when air, water, or land get dirty.**

pond a small body of fresh water *(page B43)* **The bird lives in a pond.**

position the place where something is *(page F8)* **The cat's position is inside the box.**

predict use what you know to tell what will happen *(page A44)* **You predict that the seed will grow.**

properties how something feels, looks, smells, tastes, or sounds *(page E8)* **These things have different properties.**

pull moves something closer to you *(page F6)* **You can move something with a pull.**

push moves something away from you *(page F6)* **You can move something with a push.**

R

recycle to turn old things into new things *(page D47)* **You can recycle old paper to make new paper.**

reduce to use less of something *(page D48)* **The girl reduces the use of paper towels.**

repel to push away *(page F35)*
These magnets repel each other.

reptiles animals with dry skin that is covered with scales *(page B18)*
A turtle is a reptile.

reuse to use something again *(page D46)* **The milk carton is being reused as a bird feeder.**

rocks nonliving things from Earth *(page D6)* **These rocks are different.**

roots plant parts that take in water *(page A32)* **This plant has many roots.**

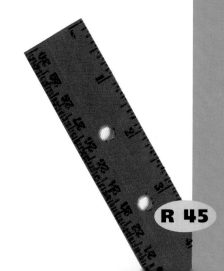

ruler measures how long, how tall, or how big around something is *(page E14)* **You can use a ruler to measure things.**

season a time of the year *(page C40)*
Spring is the season after winter.

seed the part of a plant that can
grow into new plants *(page A42)*
These seeds look different.

seedling a young plant *(page A46)*
This is a bean seedling.

senses what you use to find
out about the world around you
(page A6) **The girls use the sense
of touch.**

shelter a place where animals
can live and be safe *(page B7)*
This animal uses a tree for shelter.

sink to fall to the bottom *(page E41)*
Some solids sink in water.

soil Soil has tiny bits of rock and dead plants and animals in it. *(page D12)* **Soil has living and nonliving things in it.**

solid matter that has a shape of its own *(page E12)* **An apple is a solid.**

spring the season after winter *(page C40)* **People plant gardens in spring.**

star objects in the sky that glow and make their own light *(page C6)* **The Sun is a star.**

stem plant part through which water and food move *(page A36)* **This stem has thorns.**

stem

summer the season after spring *(page C42)* **It can be very hot in summer.**

T

tadpoles young frogs *(page B24)*
This is a tadpole.

temperature how warm or
cool something is *(page C7)*
The temperature here is hot.

trunk the stem of a tree *(page A37)*
This trunk is thick and rough.

V

vibrate to move back and forth
quickly *(page F42)* **The strings vibrate.**

W

weather what the air is like
outside *(page C28)* **The weather
here is sunny and hot.**

wind moving air *(page C28)*
The wind blows here.

winter the season after fall
(page C48) **It is winter here.**

Credits

Cover Design and Illustration: Robert Brook Allen
Cover Photos: bear cub: W. Perry Conway/Corbis; bkgrd: honeycomb Ralph Clevenger/Corbis

Illustrations: Batelman: p. R19; Rachel Geswaldo: p. R33; Wallace Keller: p. F9; Rob Schuster: pp. R20, R21; Wendy Wax: pp. Who's a Scientist cover, E06-E07; Ted Williams: pp. R17, R18; Josie Yee: pp. S4, C18-C19, C30-C31, D19. Rachel Geswaldo: p. R33;

Photography Credits: All photographs are by MacMillan/McGraw-Hill School Division (MMSD) David Mager for MMSD, Ken Karp for MMSD, Michael Groen for MMSD, and John Serafin for MMSD, except as noted below:

Contents: iv: l. Orion Press, Index Stock Imagery; b. Dominque Brud/Dembinsky Photo Assoc. v: l. Carl Purcell, Words and Pictures; l. inset Pictor; b. James Carmichael/Image Bank. vi: l. Stephen Simpson, FPG International; b. Photo Library International/Photo Researchers, Inc. vii: l. J. A. Kraulis, Masterfile; b. Diane J. Ali/Bruce Coleman, Inc. viii: l. Dave Starrett, Masterfile; ix: l. Stone/Cosmo Condina

Who's a Scientist: cover: m. David Coleman/Stock Boston; b.l. Jim Cummins/FPG International; t.l. Bob Daemmrich/Bob Daemmrich Photo, Inc.; b.r. Lawrence Migdale/Stock Boston. S1: b. Patrice Ceisel/Stock Boston; Tim Flach/Tony Stone Images. S4: inset Bill Aron/Photo Edit; bkgrd Rex Butcher/Bruce Coleman, Inc.. S5: Corbis. S7: bkgrd Don Mason/The Stock Market. S8: b.r. Tom Brakefield/Bruce Coleman, Inc.

National Geographic Unit Opener A: A0: Orion Press, Index Stock Imagery; A1: bkgrd Stone/Jake Rajs ; inset Stone/Davies & Starr Inc.;. **Unit A:** A2-A3: Jim Battles/Dembinsky Photo Assoc.. A4: inset, Howard L. Garrett/Dembinsky Photo Assoc.; b. Lawrence Migdale. A4-A5: bkgrd Michelle Burgess/Stock Boston. A6: Dan Dempster/Dembinsky Photo Assoc. A8: t.r. Mark E. Gibson/Dembinsky Photo Assoc.; b.l. Phyllis Picardi/Stock Boston. A9: Bob Daemmrich/Stock Boston. A10-A11: bkgrd, John Cancalosi/DRK Photo. A12: t.r. Bob Daemmrich/Stock Boston; inset, DPA/Dembinsky Photo Assoc.; b. Pascal Quittemelle/Stock Boston. A13: b.r. Stephen Frisch/Stock Boston; m.l. Felicia Martinez/PhotoEdit; t.r. Mark A. Schneider/Dembinsky Photo Assoc. A15: m.l. Robert P. Falls/Bruce Coleman, Inc. A18-A19: Kitney & Carmen Miller/Liaison. A20-A21: bkgrd Frans Lemmens/Image Bank. A22: t.l. Mark C. Burnett/Stock Boston; b.r. Bob Daemmrich/Stock Boston. A22-A23: bkgrd Lee Foster/Bruce Coleman, Inc. A24: b.l. Dominique Braud/Dembinsky Photo Assoc.; l. Darrell Gulin/DRK Photo.; m. William Johnson/Stock Boston. A25: t.r. Jeff Foott/DRK Photo; b.l. Bob Gurr/DRK Photo; m.r. Bill Lea/Dembinsky Photo Assoc.. A26-A27: bkgrd, Michael Newman/PhotoEdit. A28 : t. Bob Gibbons/Photo Researchers, Inc.; bkgrd Susanna Price/DK. A30-A31: G. R. Roberts/Photo Researchers, Inc.. A32: Dwight Kuhn. A32-A33: bkgrd, Maximillian Stock Ltd/Photo Researchers, Inc.. A33: inset, Rosenfeld Images /Photo Researchers, Inc.. A34-A35: Dwight Kuhn. A36: l. Dwight Kuhn. A36-A37: bkgrd, Bill Lea/Dembinsky Photo Assoc. A37: t.l. David R. Frazier/Photo Researchers, Inc.; b. Bill Gallery/Stock Boston. A38: l. Andrew McRobb/DK. A39: inset, Tom Bean/DRK Photo; m.l. William Johnson/Stock Boston; b.l. Breck P. Kent/Earth Scenes; t.l. Felicia Martinez/PhotoEdit; t.r. Felicia Martinez/PhotoEdit. A40-A41: E. R. Degginger/Dembinsky Photo Assoc. A41: r. Spencer Grant/PhotoEdit; inset, Lynn M. Stone/DRK Photo. A43: m., inset, E. R. Degginger/Dembinsky Photo Assoc.; inset, Jeff Dunn/Stock Boston; b.l. Dwight Kuhn. A44: m. Patricia Lanza/Bruce Coleman, Inc.. A46: l. Kim Taylor/DK. A46-A47: Kim Taylor/DK. A48: m.r. E. R. Degginger/Dembinsky Photo Assoc.; inset Marcia Griffen/Earth Scenes. A49: inset R. J. Erwin/Photo Researchers, Inc.; r. Scott T. Smith/Dembinsky Photo Assoc. A54: Bettman/CORBIS. A55: Bettman/CORBIS.

National Geographic Unit Opener B: B0: © Charlie Heidecker/Visuals Unlimited; B1: bkgrd Carl Purcell, Words and Pictures; inset Pictor; **Unit B:** B2 - B3: Andy Rouse. B4-B5: Ron Croucher/Nature Photographers Ltd. B6: b. Tony Stone Images; t.l. U. & J. Schimmelpfen/Natural Selection. B7: b.r. Brian Kenney/Brian Kenney; t.r. Kim Taylor, Jane Burton/DK. B8: Mark Newman/Stock Connection. B9: t. DK; m.l. Karl Shone/DK; m.r. Ron Spomer/Visuals Unlimited, Inc. B10: Brian Kenney; inset, Fritz Prenzel/Animals Animals. B11: m. PhotoDisc; t.r. Gerry Ellis/ENP Images; m.l. Robert Maier/Animals Animals; b.l. Ken Usami/PhotoDisc; b.r. J. & P. Wegner/Animals Animals. B12: t.r. S. Dalton/Animals Animals; m.l. Lynn Stone/Animals Animals. B12-B13: m. M. Harvey/DRK Photo. B13: t.r. The Cousteau Society/Image Bank. B14: m. PhotoDisc; b.r. Tim Flach/Tony Stone Images; bkgrd, Michael Fogden/DRK Photo; t.r. Allen Blake Sheldon/Animals Animals. B16: b.l. Mary Clay/Masterfile; t.l. Gordon & Cathy Illg/Animals Animals; t.r. Frank Oberia/Tony Stone Images; m.r. Jerry Young/DK. B17: b. M. Gibbs/Animals Animals. B18: b.r. James Carmichael/Image Bank; b.l. Grant Heilman/Grant Heilman Photography; t.r. Robert Maier/Animals Animals. B19: m.l. Grant Heilman/Grant Heilman Photography; t.r. Kim Taylor/DK; b.r. Kim Taylor/DK. B20: t.l. Superstock. B22-B23: Jane Burton/DK; t. Jane Burton/DK; b.r. John Daniels/DK; b.l., b.m., b.r.m. Barrie Watts/DK. B24-B25: b.r. George Bernard/Animals Animals; b.l., b.m., m. Jane Burton/Bruce Coleman, Inc.; bkgrd, George Grall/National Geographic Society; t.r. Zig Leszczynski/Animals Animals; b.l. O. S. F. /Animals Animals. B26: m.l. Superstock; t.l. Alan Carruthers/Photo Researchers, Inc.; m.r. Murray Wilson/Omni-Photo Communications. B30 - B31: David Dennis/Animals Animals. B32: Betty K. Bruce/Animals Animals; inset J. C. Carton/Bruce Coleman, Inc.; m.l. Gary Meszaros/Bruce Coleman, Inc. B34: b.r. Stanley Breeden/DRK Photo; M.R.J. Erwin/DRK Photo; b.l. Stephen J. Krasemann/DRK Photo. B34-B35: Michael Gadomski/Earth Scenes. B35: Tom Brakefield/DRK Photo. B36: m.r. John Cancalosi/Peter Arnold, Inc.; t.r. Jerry L. Ferrara/Photo Researchers, Inc.; t.l. Belinda Wright/DRK Photo; m. Belinda Wright/DRK Photo. B36-B37: Alan G. Nelson/Animals Animals. B37: t.l. Stephen J. Krasemann/DRK Photo; t.r. Richard La Val/Animals Animals; m. J. H. Robinson/Photo Researchers, Inc. B38: E. R. Degginger/Animals Animals. B40-B41: b. Tom Brakefield/Bruce Coleman, Inc.; m. Ken Cole/Animals Animals; t.l. Eastcott/Momatiuk/Animals Animals; b. Darrell Gulin/DRK Photo; m. Doug Wechsler/Earth Science. B42: b. David Hall; t. Robert C. Hermed/Photo Researchers, Inc.. B43: b.l. William Leonard/DRK Photo; inset, Maslowski/Photo Researchers, Inc.; t. Terry Whittaker/Photo Researchers, Inc.. B44: Leonard Lee Rue III/DRK Photo. B45: m. Wayne Lankinen/DRK Photo; t.l. Wayne Lynch/DRK Photo; b. Joe McDonald/DRK Photo. B47: t.r. Michael Fogden/DRK Photo; b.r. David Hall. B48-B49: b. Tim Davis/Photo Researchers, Inc.; m.l. Bill Lea/Dembinsky Photo Assoc.; t.r. Bill Lea/Dembinsky Photo Assoc.; b.r. George Schaller/Bruce Coleman, Inc.. B50: m. Rapho-DeSazo/Photo Researchers, Inc. B54: Reuters/ Weinstein/Field Museum /Archive Photos. B55: Bob Burch/Bruce Coleman, Inc.

National Geographic Unit Opener C: C0: Stephen Simpson, FPG International; C1: Stone/Jack Dykinga; **Unit C:** C2: E. R. Degginger/Bruce Coleman, Inc.. C4: Stan Osolinski/Dembinsky Photo Assoc.. C5: tr Tom Salyer/Silver Image. C5: bl Tom Salyer/Silver Image. C5: br Tom Salyer/Silver Image. C6-C7: b.r. David R. Frazier/Photo Researchers, Inc.; b. Darrell Gulin/DRK Photo; Sakura/Black Sheep. C8: b.l. Sakura/Black Sheep. C8-C9: Tony Stone Images. C9: b.r. Warren Bolster/Tony Stone Images. C10: David Nunuk/Photo Researchers, Inc. C12: m. S. Nielsen/DRK Photo; r. S. Nielsen/DRK Photo; l. S. Nielsen/DRK Photo. C13: m. S. Nielsen/DRK Photo; b.l. S. Nielsen/DRK Photo. C14-C15: Jerry Schad/Photo Researchers, Inc. C16: r. WorldSat International /Photo Researchers, Inc. C18: b. Photo Library International /Photo Researchers, Inc.. C20: m. Spencer Grant/Photo Edit. C22: Tom Salyer/Silver Image. C24-C25: Jeremy Woodhouse/DRK Photo. C26: Tom McCarthy/PhotoEdit. C28: b. Mark E. Gibson/DRK Photo; t.l. Malcolm Hanes/Bruce Coleman, Inc.. C29: m. Frank Krahmer/Bruce Coleman, Inc.; l. Jeremy Woodhouse/DRK Photo. C32-C33: Larry Mishkar/Dembinsky Photo Assoc. C34: Kim Heacox/DRK Photo. C35: t.r. American Red Cross/Photo Researchers, Inc.; m. Tom Bean/DRK Photo; bkgrd Howard Bluestein/Photo Researchers, Inc. C36: l. Christian Grzimek/Photo Researchers, Inc.; m. Jeff Lepore/Photo Researchers, Inc. C37: t.l. Melinda Berge/Bruce Coleman, Inc. t. Bonnie Sue/Photo Researchers, Inc. C38: Susan Smetana/Dembinsky Photo Assoc.. C40: t.r. E. R. Degginger/Photo Researchers, Inc.; b.l. Frank Krahmer/Bruce Coleman, Inc.. C40-C41: t. Michael P. Gadomski/Photo Researchers, Inc. C41: b. Mark E. Gibson/DRK Photo; m. Darrell Gulin/DRK Photo. C42: inset, Johnny's Selected Seeds, Albion, ME; t. David Madison/Bruce Coleman, Inc. C42-C43: b.l. Yva/John Momatiuk/Eastcott/Photo Researchers, Inc. C44: David Falconer/DRK Photo. C46: b. Mark E. Gibson/DRK Photo. C46-C47: m. Stephen G. Maka/DRK Photo. C47: t.r. Tom & Pat Leeson/Photo Researchers, Inc.; b. Tom & Pat Leeson/DRK Photo. C48: m. D. Cavagnaro/DRK Photo; b.l. John Gerlach/DRK Photo. C49: m. Gerard Fuehrer/DRK Photo; t. Norman Owen Tomalin/Bruce Coleman, Inc.; t.l. Norman Owen Tomalin/Bruce Coleman, Inc. C50-C51: m. Jeff Greenberg/Stock Boston. C54-C55: Warren Faidley/Weatherstock.

National Geographic Unit Opener D: D0: Stuart Dee, Image Bank; D1: J. A. Kraulis, Masterfile; **Unit D:** D2-D3: Nancy Sefton/Photo Researchers, Inc. D4: Lawrence Migdale. D6-D7: b. Jay Lurie/Bruce Coleman, Inc. D7: (from top) Joyce Photography/Photo Researchers, Inc.; Mark A. Schneider/Dembinsky Photo Assoc.; Ed Degginger/Brian Kenney; Biophoto Assoc./Photo Researchers, Inc.; Mark A. Schneider/Dembinsky Photo Assoc.. D8: bkgrd Bruce Esbin/Omni-Photo Comm.; b. Timothy O'Keefe/Bruce Coleman, Inc. D9: m.r. John D. Cunningham/Visuals Unlimited, Inc.; t.l. Richard Hutchings/PhotoEdit; t.r. Stephen McBrady/PhotoEdit; m. Tom McCarthy/PhotoEdit; b.r. S. McCutcheon/Visuals Unlimited, Inc.; b.l. David Young-Wolff/PhotoEdit. D10-D11: bkgrd George H. Harrison/Bruce Coleman, Inc. D12: Photo Researchers, Inc. D13: t.l. Michael Black/Bruce Coleman, Inc.; t.l. inset Phil Degginger/Bruce Coleman, Inc.; m.l. Ron Sherman/Ron Sherman; m.l. inset Glenn M. Oliver/Visuals Unlimited, Inc.; b.r. M. Timothy O'Keefe/Bruce Coleman, Inc.; b.r. inset Deborah Davis/Photo Edit. D14: t.r. Bob Daemmrich/Bob Daemmrich Photo, Inc.. D14-D15: Willard Clay/Dembinsky Photo Assoc.. D15: inset E. R. Degginger/Photo Researchers, Inc.; T. Hans Reinhard/Bruce Coleman, Inc. D16: inset Nicholas Devore/Bruce Coleman, Inc. D16-D17: bkgrd Alan Kearney/FPG International. D18: l. Janis Burger/Bruce Coleman, Inc. D18-D19: r. Larry Blank/Visuals Unlimited, Inc. D19: Michael James/Photo Researchers, Inc. D20: m.l. Dennis McDonald/Photo Edit; t.r. David Young-Wolff/PhotoEdit. D20-D21: bkgrd Janine Pestel/Visuals Unlimited, Inc. D21: inset D. Pearson/Visuals Unlimited, Inc. D22-D23: bkgrd Myrleen Cate/Photo Edit. D24: t.r. PhotoDisc; b.l. Bonnioe Kamin/Photo Edit; m. Mike Welsch/Photo Edit. D24-D25: bkgrd Jack W. Dykinga/Bruce Coleman, Inc. D25: inset Mary Kate Denny/Photo Edit; t.r. Richard Smith/Dembinsky Photo Assoc.. D26-D27: bkgrd Lawrence Migdale. D28: t.l. Diane J. Ali/Bruce Coleman, Inc.; m.l. M. W. Black/Bruce Coleman, Inc.; t.r. Tony Freeman/PhotoEdit; b. Michael Newman/Photo Edit. D29: b.r. Bruce Coleman, Inc.; m.l. E. R. Degginger/Dembinsky Photo Assoc.; m. Michael Newman/Photo Edit; b. Mary M. Steinbacher/Photo Edit. D30: b.l. D. Cavagnaro/Visuals Unlimited, Inc.; t. Simon Fraser Science Photo Library/Photo Researchers, Inc.; b. David Young-Wolff/Photo Edit. D30-D31: Jock Montgomery/Bruce Coleman, Inc.. D31: t.l. Andrew Dalsimer/Bruce Coleman, Inc.; b. John Elk III/Bruce Coleman, Inc.; t.r. Mark Richards/Photo Edit. D32: Culver Pictures. D36-D37: Bruce M. Herman/Photo Researchers, Inc.. D38-D39: bkgrd Steve McCutcheon/Visuals Unlimited, Inc.. D40: inset Phil Degginger/Phil Degginger. D40-D41: Georg Gerster/Photo Researchers, Inc.. D42: l. John Mielcarek/Dembinsky Photo Assoc.; r. Dick Thomas/Visuals Unlimited, Inc.. D43: Eunice Harris/Photo Researchers, Inc.. D44-d45: John Elk/Stock Boston. D46: t. Jeff Greenberg/Visuals Unlimited, Inc.. D47: t. Myrleen Ferguson/Photo Edit. D49: m. Bill Bachman/Photo Researchers, Inc.. D54: m. The Granger Collection; b.l. The Granger Collection, New York; bkgrd Layne Kennedy/Corbis. D55: m.r. Layne Kennedy/Corbis.

National Geographic Unit Opener E: E0: © Philip Gould/CORBIS; E1: Dave Starrett, Masterfile; **Unit E:** E2 - E3: David Sams/Stock Boston. E4-E5: Jeff Greenberg/Stock Boston. E8: l. Jeanne White/Photo Researchers, Inc.. E16: t.r. Barbara Alper/Stock Boston; b. Robert Maier/Animals Animals. E22-E23: bkgrd, Superstock. E30-E31: Craig Tuttle/The Stock Market. E38-E39: bkgrd, Henryk Kaiser/Leo de Wye Stock Photo Agency. E44-E45: bkgrd, Tom Stewart/The Stock Market. E46: t.l. The Stock Market. E46-E47: m. Robert Essel/The Stock Market. E47: t.l. George Kamper/Tony Stone Images; r. Charles D. Winters/Photo Researchers, Inc. E48: l. Superstock; b.l. Bill Bonoszewski/Visuals Unlimited, Inc. E48-E49: t.r. Gerben Oppermans/Tony Stone Images.

National Geographic Unit Opener F: F0: Stone/Cosmo Condina; F1: Stone/Cosmo Condina; **Unit F:** F2-F3: Lori Adamski Peek/Tony Stone Images. F4-F5: Myrleen Cate/Photo Edit; bkgrd Orion Press/Natural Selection. F10-F11: bkgrd Dennis O'Clair/Tony Stone Images. F14-F15: bkgrd /Superstock. F16 : b. Spencer Grant/Photo Edit; inset ,MichaelNewman/Photo Edit. F16 - F17: bkgrd David R. Frazier/David R. Frazier Photolibrary. F17: t.l. Robert E. Daemmrich/Tony Stone Images. F18: l. David Madison/Tony Stone Images. F18-F19: m. Superstock; t.r. Margaret Kois/The Stock Market. F19: t.l. Lori Adamski Peek/Tony Stone Images. F40-F41: bkgrd Superstock; inset George Disario/The Stock Market. F42: l. Bill Aron/PhotoEdit; m. Tom McCarthy/Photo Edit. F43: b.r. Laura Dwight/; t. Lawrence Migdale. F44: Mark Downey/Viesti Associates, Inc.; b.l. Robert Fried/Stock Boston. F46: t. Jeff Greenberg/David R. Frazier Photolibrary; b. J. Barry O'Rourke/The Stock Market. F47: b.r. David R. Frazier Photolibrary; t.r. A. Ramey/Photo Edit. F48: b. Andy Cox/Tony Stone Images; m. Denis Scott/The Stock Market. F49: David R. Frazier Photolibrary; b.l. John Lamb/Tony Stone Images. F54: b.r. Robert Holmgren. F55: Robert Holmgren.

Science and Health Handbook: R8: l. J. C. Carton/Bruce Coleman, Inc.; b.r. E. R. Degginger/Bruce Coleman, Inc.; r. Phil Degginger/Bruce Coleman, Inc.. R14: PhotoDisc. R28: t.l. Jim Whitmer/FPG International. R29: PhotoDisc; b.l. Laura Dwight/Peter Arnold, Inc.. R31: Myrleen Ferguson/Photo Edit. R32: Jerry Schad/Photo Researchers, Inc. R34: t.r. Adam Smith/FPG International; b.l. Ed Wheeler/The Stock Market.

Photographs by Roman Sapecki and/or Lew Lause for MMSD: pp. R27; R28:m. & b.; R30: t; R31: b.

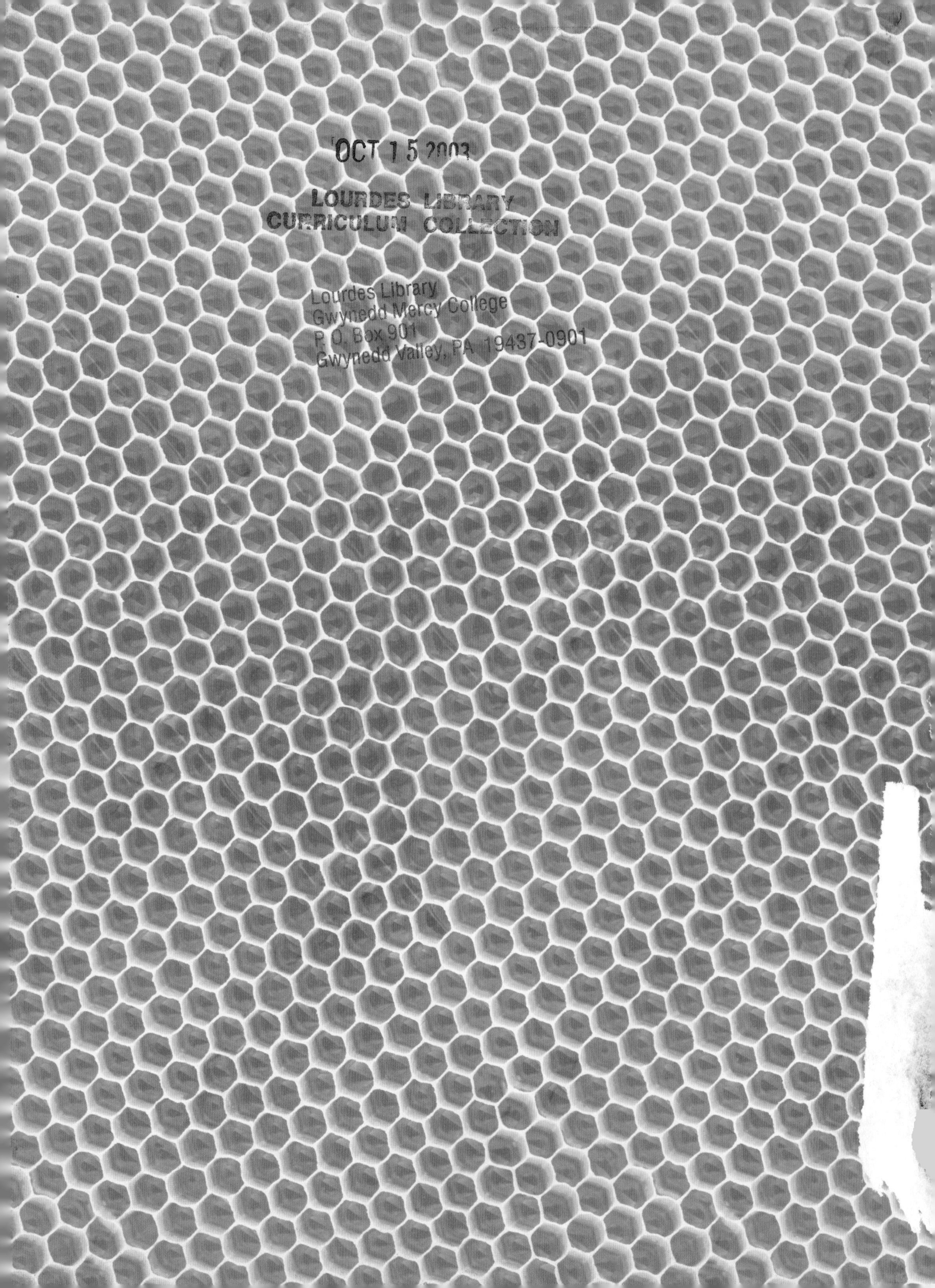